Praise for *Box of Bu*

"With *Box of Butterflies*, Roma Downey has created a beautiful and personal testimony to the presence of God in our lives and in our world. Her book is filled with stories and poems and quotations that give us hope in God's healing power and love. Roma talks personally about her own sorrows and struggles, and her book will offer consolation to others, helping them face their troubles with renewed courage and trust in God."

—Most Reverend José H. Gomez, Archbishop of Los Angeles

"I have known my 'Angel friend,' Roma, for decades. We met when I guest-starred on her TV show, *Touched by an Angel*. We became friends then and we still are, today, because Roma is the REAL THING. She loves Jesus with a rare purity, and His love radiates from within her. You will love her new book. It will touch you and move you and strengthen you."

—Kathie Lee Gifford, *TODAY* show

"I've long said that the happiest people don't have the best of everything, they just make the best of everything. In *Box of Butterflies*, Roma shares personal struggles and the perspectives that have helped her overcome. Roma will help you find the strength within to go to heights you never imagined."

—Tony Robbins, *New York Times* bestselling author of *Unshakeable*

"Roma Downey is one of the most generous, compassionate, and all-around amazing people I have ever met. She's never too busy or too important to care about the person in front of her. I can't think of a clearer indicator of greatness than that. Somehow, she has managed to capture her humanness, empathy, and humility in the pages of her book *Box of Butterflies*. Reading this book is like having a face-to-face chat with Roma herself. You'll come away refreshed, comforted, and inspired to live with deeper peace and greater faith. I hope you enjoy it as much as I do!"

—Judah Smith, pastor and *New York Times* bestselling author of *Jesus Is _____*.

"This book gladdens the heart, nudges the memory, and lightly touches the soul with inspiration. *Box of Butterflies* is an invitation to hope, joy, and insight in the tradition of the Irish bards."

—Cardinal Donald Wuerl, Archbishop of Washington

"God promises us in His Word that we will not be overcome, but rather that we are overcomers. My friend, Roma, embodies that truth. Despite loss and heartache, she chooses to make God's goodness greater than her circumstances. Her personal story and the Scriptures she shares in *Box of Butterflies* will encourage you with reminders of God's love and presence in your everyday life."

—Christine Caine, founder, A21 and Propel Women

"Like an opened box of butterflies, Roma Downey's stories flew off the page and filled my heart with hope. Find a quiet spot and journey with Roma from the war-torn streets of Northern Ireland to the shores of sunny Malibu. As you do, you just might see the exquisite design in your own life. God is at work! *Box of Butterflies* is proof."

—Karen Kingsbury, #1 *New York Times* bestselling author

"The moment I read the first word, I was instantly connected and inspired. This book brings inspiration and clarity to life's journey. Dive in and swim in the wisdom. 💯 "

—LL COOL J

"When someone gives you hope in your life, it is priceless! *Box of Butterflies* is a profound collection of God's great promises that are overflowing with hope! As you learn them, share them with the world!"

—Dr. Ronnie Floyd, president, National Day of Prayer, senior pastor, Cross Church, and immediate past president, Southern Baptist Convention

"This inspiring book reveals how our struggles generate new strength, and even become the means by which we grow in the Spirit. Read Roma Downey's text slowly, savor it—let it sink into your heart. I warmly recommend it to anyone weighed down by the difficulties of life."

—Bishop Robert Barron, Auxiliary Bishop of Los Angeles

"It's said that tears cleanse the windows of the soul, and you'll find several refreshingly soul-cleansing moments within the pages of this book. You'll also find it a deeply inspiring and motivating read, authored not by an 'angel' but by a faithful overcomer who's willing to honestly share her life's tragedies and triumphs. A beautiful book written by a beautiful person."

—Laurie Crouch, Trinity Broadcasting Network

For my beautiful daughter,
Reilly . . .
the little girl who grew
up to be my best friend

Box *of* Butterflies

Discovering the Unexpected Blessings All Around Us

ROMA DOWNEY

HOWARD BOOKS

ATRIA

New York   London   Toronto   Sydney   New Delhi

An Imprint of Simon & Schuster, Inc.
1230 Avenue of the Americas
New York, NY 10020

First Howard Books/Atria Paperback edition February 2022

HOWARD BOOKS **/ATRIA** PAPERBACK and colophon are trademarks of Simon & Schuster, Inc.

For information about special discounts for bulk purchases, please contact Simon & Schuster Special Sales at 1-866-506-1949 or business@simonandschuster.com.

The Simon & Schuster Speakers Bureau can bring authors to your live event. For more information or to book an event, contact the Simon & Schuster Speakers Bureau at 1-866-248-3049 or visit our website at www.simonspeakers.com.

Manufactured in China

3   5   7   9   10   8   6   4   2

Library of Congress Cataloging-in-Publication Data has been applied for.

ISBN 978-1-5011-5093-7 (hardcover)
ISBN 978-15011-5106-4 (paperback)
ISBN 978-1-5011-5096-8 (ebook)

CONTENTS

Dear Readers,

My darling Roma has written this very special book, called *Box of Butterflies*. I couldn't be more proud of her, and I delight in sharing it with you. Whether you bought this book as a beautiful gift for yourself or for someone you love, I know you will be truly touched by the Spirit that exudes from its pages as Roma shares the beauty of her soul and the sweetness of her spirit. You'll find great warmth and wisdom within.

I feel so fortunate to have had Roma in my life for all these years. If you don't already know it, God was the one who brought us together many years ago, when we played angels on our beloved television show *Touched by an Angel*. The relationship between the angels Tess and Monica was much like the one that developed between Roma and me off camera—authentic, caring, loving, protective, and true. We are soul sisters, and it is as if we have known each other forever. As you will learn in these pages, she has become my daughter, and I am her mama. I've loved seeing her grow into the beautiful mother, wife, producer, author, and extraordinary woman she is today.

Like many of us, Roma has experienced terrible loss and struggle in her life. But like the caterpillar that uses the darkness of the cocoon to transform into a butterfly, Roma has taken the darkness of life's challenges and, with God's help and grace, used those same trials to bring light to our world. Roma has, indeed, earned her wings.

Roma came to America from Ireland with nothing but a prayerful heart full of hope and a mind full of dreams. She has had a wonderful career in Hollywood but has remained strong in her faith and continues to glorify God by creating projects for Him. In this book, Roma shares stories about her journey, the trials and the triumphs, the joys and the sorrows. I am certain that her story, combined with the beautiful poetry and Scripture she has selected, will inspire hope, restore broken faith, and remind us all that God loves us. That we are never alone. We are all connected, and our loving God and His angels are always standing by, watching over us.

May this *Box of Butterflies* be a blessing to all of you, as Roma has been to me.

God bless you,
Della Reese

I Have Decided

I have decided to find myself a home
in the mountains, somewhere high up
where one learns to live peacefully in
the cold and silence. It's said that
in such a place certain revelations may
be discovered. That what the spirit
reaches for may be eventually felt, if not
exactly understood. Slowly, no doubt. I'm
not talking about a vacation.

Of course at the same time I mean to
stay exactly where I am.

Are you following me?

Mary Oliver

INTRODUCTION

I love the poems of Mary Oliver—like the one you just read—and you'll find a few scattered throughout these pages. There is something about the beauty and honesty of her poems that echoes the prayers of my heart. She reminds me of the simplicity of faith, of how God's image is reflected in nature all around us, and that when we are quiet, when we connect to the stillness within ourselves, we can hear Him speak.

I hope that within the pages of this book you'll find moments like that. Moments when your heart flutters as it makes a connection, like finally being able to recall a distant memory, moments when you are filled with the relief of remembering that you are not alone and that God's loving presence is all around you.

I've been a person of faith my whole life. I was raised in a household where it was always the right time for a prayer, where gratitude to God for His blessings was part of the everyday fabric of our lives. I lost my mother suddenly when I was only ten, and our faith became even more essential as my family leaned on each other and God to get us through that difficult and painful time.

I remember the first time I went with my father to visit my mother's gravesite, not long after she passed. We'd brought some pansies to plant by her gravestone. My mother loved pansies. She used to say she thought they looked like little butterflies.

As we stood there on the breezy hillside praying, a butterfly flew right in front of us, dancing on the wind. And my dad said, "Would you look at that! That wee butterfly could be your mother's spirit right there."

As a young girl of ten, the idea that a beautiful butterfly could represent my precious mom gave me great comfort. I have always felt that that butterfly was a gift from God, a reminder of His loving presence. Since that day, butterflies have appeared to me throughout my life, bringing with them peace and reassurance. I always see them as a remembrance of my mother and a sign from God that even though we may feel so incredibly alone sometimes, He is always there.

Now, some people tell me, "Well, Roma, you live in California; it's sunny and your garden is full of flowers, so of course you see butterflies all the time!" And while yes, that is true, I don't see only physical butterflies. Over the course of my life I have

We delight in the beauty of the butterfly, but rarely admit the changes it has gone through to achieve that beauty.

MAYA ANGELOU

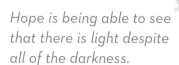

seen butterflies appear in all sorts of unexpected places. A truck will drive by on a rainy city street with a butterfly painted on the side; or in the

Hope is being able to see that there is light despite all of the darkness.

DESMOND TUTU

midst of a long mountain drive, a butterfly will show up on a billboard, on a piece of jewelry in a store, or as a tattoo on a waitress's neck as we stop for some food. I can't explain it, but throughout my life at the precise moments I need a sign of hope, I see a butterfly, and it always serves as a reminder of God's love and reassurance that I am not alone.

If you visit my home, you'll see paintings of butterflies, butterflies on mugs and napkins and pillows and more. Butterflies and angels with wings to fly. Because to me, the butterfly is not just a sign of God's presence but also a symbol of the promise that we all hold within. A butterfly begins its life as a simple caterpillar, creeping and crawling along the ground. And yet that is just its beginning. Through the process of metamorphosis, through the patience and darkness of the cocoon, this little caterpillar emerges on the other side as a stunning butterfly, a creature with wings and the ability to fly.

I once heard a story of a little boy who saw a cocoon and was so anxious to help the butterfly emerge that he got a small pair of manicure scissors so that he could help cut the butterfly out. What he didn't know was that it is through the process of emerging from the cocoon on its own that the butterfly gains the power to fly. It's the very struggle to push out of the cocoon that gives its wings their strength. Without that process, without the struggle, the butterfly isn't ready to fly. To soar.

I know that this life can be filled with sorrow. We all experience loss and heartbreak. But oh, if we can just remember that in the struggle our wings become stronger. We can get through even the hardest times, and one day we will fly.

We sometimes forget this. We think we will always be caterpillars crawling along the ground or bound in a cocoon. But we all hold the potential to become something else. There is always the chance for rebirth.

One year, for Valentine's Day, my husband, Mark, took me out to our patio, which overlooks the Pacific Ocean in Malibu, where we live. He handed me a large, exquisitely designed box with a fragrant gardenia on top. I was surprised by how light it was, and I must have looked puzzled. Mark smiled and told me to just open it carefully. So I took the lid off gently, and out flew fifty butterflies. I gasped as I watched them ascend into the sky. My heart filled with joy and delight and my eyes filled with tears. I turned to look at Mark, my heart overflowing with gratitude. My lovely husband had given me a box of butterflies, knowing that for me, the butterfly is a sign of God's grace, God's presence.

It was the dearest gift I could have received.

It reminded me of the blessings of my life and the little lessons I have learned along the way, and so I decided to call this book *Box of Butterflies*. It is my prayer that each page of this book is a butterfly for you. A reminder that God is with you. That He will never leave you or forsake you. And that no matter how dark the cocoon may sometimes seem, there is always light on the other side. The struggle means your wings are growing and being strengthened. Have faith. There are angels watching over you.

Back in 1994, I was an out-of-work actress looking for a job. I had been in Los Angeles for just over a year and was still waiting for my big break. To be honest, I had never really intended to come to L.A. and try to make it as a TV actress. I was classically trained in London and had moved to New York with my heart set on Broadway. My dream came true in the early 1990s, when I was cast on Broadway alongside Sir Rex Harrison in a revival of Somerset Maugham's *The Circle*. Yet much to my surprise, some television producers saw my performance and called me in to read for an NBC miniseries called *A Woman Named Jackie*, a six-hour film about the life of Jackie Kennedy.

My agency sent me the script, and I read the first of six episodes. The material

> *He who is not courageous enough to take risks will accomplish nothing in life.*
> MUHAMMAD ALI

was compelling, but I didn't know what character they were thinking of for me. I called my agent to ask. He said with a laugh, "Well, the title role, of course."

My jaw dropped. It was hard to imagine me, an Irish woman, playing this iconic American beauty. And yet I booked the role, and the series went on to win the Emmy for best miniseries that year. On the heels of its success, I decided to pack my bags again and move to Hollywood to see what other TV or film opportunities might arise.

The idea of moving to Los Angeles filled me with trepidation. I hardly knew anyone on the West Coast, and I did not even know how to drive a car. But I prayed and felt certain I should go. I decided I would try it out; if I did not like it, I could always go back to New York. I felt strongly that if I didn't give it a chance, I would always regret not having tried. So in spite of being afraid of what lay ahead and with no certainty of outcome, I got on a plane at JFK and flew west.

It was pilot season—that time of year when the hope that keeps all actors in this challenging profession rises, when you think that your next big break might just be around the corner. When you hope that the perfect, special script with the perfect, special role might just show up and change your life.

> Courage is being scared to death but saddling up anyway.
>
> JOHN WAYNE

I read through a number of scripts that my agent wanted me to consider, but none was terribly appealing. And then I picked up one with the working title *Angel's Attic* (later to be retitled *Touched by an Angel*). I felt a fluttering in my stomach. I knew immediately that this was something different.

As I opened the packet and began to read, tears came to my eyes. This was the kind of material I had been looking for. The series told the story of angels who show up at crossroads in people's lives with a message of faith and love. The angels come to earth to remind people that God loves them and hasn't forgotten them.

I called my agent and told him that I wanted to come in to read for one of the roles. We booked a meeting, and a few days later they called me in to be considered for the role of Monica, one of the lead angels.

As I began preparing for the audition, I couldn't believe that this script presented me with an opportunity to play an angel and bring to life so many elements of the faith that I held dear. In addition, the two lead angels were women who shared an empathetic and loving relationship. Most of the scripts I was reading were about women in conflict, fighting over something or in competition with one another. But here were two women, two angels, who had so much love for each other. The story was inspirational and told of God's grace, not something that Hollywood or network television was necessarily known for.

As I prepared for my audition, I realized that playing the role of Monica would require a compassionate heart. And I felt deep in my soul that I had been prepared for this role by the loss I had experienced in my own life. I knew that I could relate to the very people Monica was coming to visit, that I could meet those people in their places of loss and hurt because

I had felt loss and hurt so intensely myself at such a young age. I understood then that God had been preparing me, and I'd now been given the chance to turn my pain into purpose.

When I went in to read for the part, I felt torn about how to approach my portrayal of Monica. I had, of course, worked on my American accent during the rehearsals for playing Jackie, but there was something within me that felt like the lyricism and musicality of my native Irish accent might be right for this special part of an angel. I knew it would be risky. It might cause me to lose the role. Once people hear my accent, it's often all they can hear, even when I'm speaking in an American accent. But I couldn't ignore this feeling.

The wound is the place where the Light enters you.

RUMI

I walked into the room and read my lines, as I'm sure every other actress had read them, in an American accent. It seemed to go well. But then, before I left the room, I turned around and cautiously asked if I could read it again. The producers nodded, perhaps a bit confused. And then I read Monica's lines in my native Irish brogue.

The energy in the room changed immediately. Everyone in the room could feel it. Something clicked.

As I left the audition, I thanked God for guiding me to listen to my instincts. Sure enough, I was called back for a screen test, and they requested that I read it again in my Irish accent.

A few days later, I received a call from my agent. "I have good news and bad news," he said.

"Good news first," I said.

"You booked the show!"

"That's amazing," I said. "What's the bad news?"

"If the pilot gets picked up, you have to move to Utah," he said.

I laughed and said I thought I could handle that! I had never been to Utah but had heard it was beautiful. I was so thrilled with this opportunity, the chance to play Monica, and knew that my life was going to change in huge ways.

Obviously that pilot was an answer to prayer. It was a breakout moment for me and resulted in almost a decade of creating a beautiful show and being part of a cast and crew who truly became my family.

But it became so much more than just my profession. Playing an angel for almost ten years truly changed me. It touched my heart deeply, and strengthened my faith as well.

My favorite part of each episode was filming the scene we called the "angel revelation." It came about forty minutes into the show. Monica was an undercover angel pretending to be a nurse or a doctor or a police officer, but she was truly there to help someone at an emotional crossroads. The moment always came when they broke down, feeling lost in the midst of their painful circumstances, before finally fully surrendering to God. They would cry out: "I cannot do this by myself. God help me." This was the central, emotional heart of each episode. Monica would then reveal her true identity as an angel from Almighty God. She was a messenger, and the message was this: "There is a God, He loves you, and He has a plan for your life." Before filming this scene, I would close my eyes, open my heart, and pray.

It was an emotional moment to film, but it also filled me up—so much so that I would leave the set feeling as if God had just touched me personally. This was the moment that person opened his or her eyes and felt the truth he or she had forgotten: That he or she was a special child of a loving God—a child who was loved unconditionally. That God was always there. That he or she had never been alone, despite desperate feelings of loneliness.

It was a moment of remembering.

When we are caught up in the busyness of our lives, we forget our true role in this life. When we are wrapped up in worrying about the future or are stressed about something we did in the past, we do not feel God's peace. But if we can simply stop and be in the *now*, we can remember Him. In remembering Him we come to a point of stillness and surrender. And it is in our stillness that God comes in. It is in the silence that we hear the whisper of His voice.

Be still, and know that I am God.

PSALM 46:10 (NIV)

It was such a privilege to bring that message of unconditional love to a nation full of viewers for so many years.

And in some ways, that is what I am trying to do in this book. I pray this book is a moment of remembering for *you*. A remembering of who you really are, how much God loves you, and that you are never, ever truly alone.

Before we would film each scene of revelation, we would pray as a cast and crew. My personal prayer was always, "Less of me, more of You." I pray that for this book as well. This is not about me or my life or even my faith. This is about how God has shown up in my life—and how He can show up in yours.

In these pages I'll share songs and prayers and poems that have kept me going in both the sunshine and shadows of my life. I'll share glimpses of God that I have found in the written word or in a particular image. And I pray that as you read these words, you may remember, you may awaken, you may feel God's gentle presence. And that you then may go forward, knowing that the greatest Shepherd, Companion, and Father is always by your side.

For I am the Lord your God
who takes hold of your right hand
and says to you, Do not fear;
I will help you.

ISAIAH 41:13 (NIV)

He did not say "You shall not be tormented, you shall not be troubled, you shall not be grieved," but he said, "You shall not be overcome."

JULIAN OF NORWICH

He heals the brokenhearted, and binds up their wounds.

PSALM 147:3 (NIV)

STRENGTH

one

STRENGTH

*Our wounds are often the openings into the best
and most beautiful part of us.*

DAVID RICHO

ALL MY LIFE I have been drawn to the ocean. I love the sound of the waves. The natural rhythm of the ebb and flow is like a massage for my mind and my spirit. I have always done my best thinking by the sea. And I often take my worries to the ocean's edge and quietly pray while I walk on the sand.

There is something about the vast expanse of water that helps to put my troubles in proper perspective. In the grand scheme of things, all the concerns I have or deadlines I need to meet suddenly don't seem so critical. The scale of the ocean serves as a reminder of the magnificence of God and the smallness of the things I may be worrying about. As the waves wash in and out, they remind me that this, too, shall pass. It calms me and restores me. Sometimes I stand alone on the shore and sing at the top of my voice and see my footprints on the sand. With each wave that races to the beach, I watch them gently wash away.

I did not grow up by the seaside, but Ireland is a small island surrounded on all sides by water. I grew up in the North West, and many of my childhood summers were spent in Donegal. The ocean there is wilder than the Pacific, but even when it was cold—and it was often cold—I loved being near it and found it energizing.

I need the sea because it teaches me.

PABLO NERUDA

We would go to the little seaside town of Moville on day trips or family outings, and after a full day of playing on the beach or walking along the shore toward Greencastle, we'd end up having our evening meal at a nice family-run hotel. It felt so swanky to eat out and have a waiter serve us. I now have the good fortune to eat out regularly, but back then this was a total luxury. My brother Lawrence and I would order steak and chips, and they would serve our ketchup in these little silver bowls. And as a special treat, we were allowed to order a bottle of Coca-Cola or Fanta Orange. We'd go home tired from all the sea air and meat and potatoes.

When I look back on my childhood, I know it was a happy one. We lived in a tiny row house, in a neighborhood filled with other children. It was a time when kids went out onto the streets to play. Boys had their own games, primarily soccer, while the girls would pass the time with hopscotch using an old shoe polish tin as the marker, or throwing tennis balls against the drugstore wall to the beat of a variety of rhyming songs that all the girls would sing. When wet weather drove us indoors, we'd play paper dolls and put on talent shows and play dress-up—all the games of imagination that ignited in me dreams of being an actress and living a different life.

My mother loved the theater. In another life she may have loved pursuing a career on the stage herself. It was from her that I developed my love of and passion for performing. With her encouragement, I took dance classes and music classes and singing classes and elocution classes. Yes, elocution! She would come with me and sit off to the side of the classroom, urging me on with her love and her laughter and her enthusiasm. I adored her. She was warm, gregarious, and very funny. She would have made an excellent comic actress, like an Irish Lucille Ball.

At bedtime she would lie on top of the covers on my bed, as the night slowly ushered in the darkness, singing show tunes to me as I fell asleep. Then one week shy of my eleventh birthday, my mother died of a heart attack. Her young, vibrant life was cut unexpectedly short, and my happy childhood abruptly ended.

It happened on an ordinary day. My mother, brother, and I were walking from our row house to the library nearby. Without warning, my mother collapsed in the street. She was able to get back up and sit on the side of the road while my brother ran to a neighbor's house for help. They got their car and drove us home and helped my mother to her bed.

Mom, not wanting her children to worry, kept trying to reassure us. "Oh, I've just got a wee tummy ache. Don't worry, I'll be fine with a bit of rest."

My father was summoned, as well as the doctor, and it was decided that she would go to the hospital for some tests. An ambulance arrived, but because our row house was so narrow, they couldn't fit a stretcher up the staircase to fetch her, so instead, my mother was carried down in a chair by four men. I remember her making jokes as they strapped her in and hoisted the chair, her humor making the men who carried her laugh. It is one of the last memories I have of her alive.

My brother, father, and I were standing in the doorway of what we called "the good room," and as she passed by she looked at us, smiling, and said, "Don't worry, I'll see you soon. Lawrence, you take care of your sister until I get back. Roma, you take care of your da."

We never saw her again.

The next morning, a hush descended on the household as news spread that our mother was ill, and various adults whispered as they entered and exited the house. The phone's constant ringing was the soundtrack to the tense morning. It was clear that something bad was going on.

Pretty soon my brother and I were packed up to go to the hospital with my father. I was hopeful that we were going there to bring our mother home. We entered a waiting room, a room that I remember being defined by the loud tick-tock of the clock echoing in the stressful silence.

There we sat, my father, my brother, my mother's sister Ruby, and her best friend, Maureen, who shared the same name as my mom. Eventually a doctor came in and asked my father to step outside.

And when my dad came back in, he was crying. I had never seen him cry before.

"She's gone," he said, with a quiet sob.

At first, I didn't understand. There is always a part of you that doesn't want to believe in the face of tragedy. But as I watched my father cry, I knew there was only one thing that could make him cry. My mother was dead.

Be strong and courageous. Do not be afraid or terrified because of them, for the Lord your God goes with you; he will never leave you nor forsake you.

DEUTERONOMY 31:6 (NIV)

For me, it was like the lights had been turned out and all the color of life removed.

She had been the joy in our home. She was the warm fire on a cold night; she was the cheerful word on a gloomy day. She was the center of my world, and then suddenly, in an instant, she was gone.

No more Mom sitting in the corner waiting for me, no more songs as I fell asleep, no more holding hands and running in the rain.

I often say that my father was sadness in a suit after the loss of my mother. I know he felt her absence deeply. She had been so gregarious and joyful, and laughter came very easily to her, while my father was more reserved and even a little shy. Our entire household had to recalibrate after she was gone, and for a while, we stumbled around in the dark, all of us grieving, unsure of the way forward.

This was the second tragedy for my father. He had been married before, and his first wife had died, leaving him with four children under the age of twelve to raise on his own. He met and married my mother many years later, when his four children were grown, and he had built another happy family. Yet once again, he found himself wearing the heavy mantle of widower, this time with two children under the age of twelve. His now grown children did what they could to help, but they had lives and families of their own. Because of our age differences, they were more like aunts and uncles to me, but they tried to help us feel a sense of family in the wake of another tragic loss. They, too, knew what it was to grow up without a mother.

I took my troubles to the Lord; I cried out to him, and he answered my prayer.

PSALM 120:1 (NLT)

My dad did his best to be not only a father but a mother to us as well. He didn't sing me to sleep, but every night he would lie down beside me and read poetry to me before I went to sleep. And then he would turn out the lights and make the sound of the ocean to calm me into slumber.

I look back on this painful time and remember being so confused. How could my mother be so healthy and by my side one day and then gone the next? I worried that perhaps it was my fault—if I had somehow been *more*, she would have stayed. I strove to be a good girl, so scared that if I did something wrong, my dad would be taken as well.

I remember riding home from the hospital in a taxi that horrible morning she died. I sat in the backseat with my brother, and my mother's best friend, whom we called Auntie Maureen, sat up front with the driver. It was a rainy, bleak day. I stared out the rain-flecked window, feeling so alone. And then I heard my aunt say quietly to the driver, "My best friend, Maureen O'Reilly, just died. Those are her w'anes back there." It was the first time I had heard those words spoken out loud. Without looking at each other, my brother and I reached out across the backseat of the taxi and clasped each other's hands, knowing that our lives had been changed forever.

That memory has stuck with me all these years. And, to me, that moment embodies the instinct we all have during difficult times. To reach out for someone's hand, to be reassured that no matter how painful life is, there is always someone to reach out to. A brother, a sister, a friend, or God.

Because the truth is, though we may feel so alone, we are never truly alone.

What I sometimes find astonishing is that the song my mother sang to me every night before I went to sleep is a song from the Rodgers and Hammerstein musical *Carousel*. It is called "You'll Never Walk Alone." When I was a child, listening to my mother's beautiful voice sing me to sleep, it reminded me that even after she put me to bed and closed the door and went down to the living room to be with my father, she was somehow still with me. And, of course, after her death, that song came to symbolize so much more. That no matter where I am, she will always be with me.

You'll Never Walk Alone

When you walk through a storm
Hold your head up high
And don't be afraid of the dark.
At the end of the storm is a golden sky
And the sweet silver song of a lark.

Walk on through the wind,
Walk on through the rain,
Tho' your dreams be tossed and blown.
Walk on, walk on, with hope in your heart
And you'll never walk alone,
You'll never walk alone.

Richard Rodgers and Oscar Hammerstein II

Even today, as I read those words, my eyes fill with tears. What truth lies in those lyrics. Dark and stormy times will come, but when they do, we must keep walking through the wind and the rain, our eyes fixed on where we pray the golden sky will appear.

This is the essence of faith, isn't it? To keep hold of the knowledge that this isn't the end, that there is a promise of heaven, that God can redeem even the most difficult circumstances.

Shortly after my mother died, my father shared the poem "Footprints" with me. I have carried that poem in my wallet

ever since. It talks about a person of faith looking back on her life and seeing two sets of footprints on the sand, representing that God has been by her side her entire life. But as the person looks closer, she notices that during the darkest times in her life, there is just one set of footprints. At first she reaches out to God in anger—*How could you abandon me when I needed you most?* But God gently says, *No, my dear child. For it is then that I was carrying you.*

Throughout my life, I've found that it is in those very moments of darkness that God can come in. In the dark is when His light can shine the brightest. For when we are struggling, unable to hold it all together, is when we surrender. And that is when He can finally pick us up and carry us.

Our glory is hidden in our pain, if we allow God to bring the gift of himself in our experience of it.

HENRI NOUWEN

The Lord is my shepherd, I lack nothing.

He makes me lie down in green pastures,

he leads me beside quiet waters,

he refreshes my soul.

He guides me along the right paths

for his name's sake.

Even though I walk

through the darkest valley,

I will fear no evil,

for you are with me;

your rod and your staff,

they comfort me.

You prepare a table before me

in the presence of my enemies.

You anoint my head with oil;

my cup overflows.

Surely your goodness and love will follow me

all the days of my life,

and I will dwell in the house of the Lord

forever.

Psalm 23 (NIV)

A MESSAGE IN
THE MOON

When you walk to the edge of all the light you have,
And take that first step into the darkness of the unknown,
You must believe one of two things will happen:
There will be something solid for you to stand upon,
Or, you will be taught how to fly.

PATRICK OVERTON

When I think of my father, I can see that throughout my life, he was always trying to give me wings so that I could go anywhere I wanted. He said over and over that my education would be my passport out and that I needed to work hard in school so I could go to college. He was always supportive and encouraging of my artistic desires, and when the time came to interview for college, he went with me and sat in the waiting area!

As I was preparing to leave Ireland for school in England, I began to feel anxious. This was before the Internet and cell phones, and to be so far away from my father, with no way of immediately reaching him, made me extremely nervous.

One night, just a few days before I was scheduled to leave, he took me outside to the backyard. It was a clear night with a full moon. And he said, "Roma, wherever you are in the world, that moon will be shining on you. So whenever you feel alone, always look into the night sky, and you'll be reminded of how much I love you. I'll leave a message for you in the moon."

I hugged him, so grateful for his sweet gentleness and his constant care and attention.

And as that first full moon

Education is not the filling of a pail, but the lighting of a fire.

WILLIAM BUTLER YEATS

ascended after I had settled in England, I went outside and looked up at the moon. And I felt my dad's love. It was a great comfort.

Since my mother had passed away, I had lived in fear that something might happen to Dad. If he was late coming home from work or I came home to an empty house when I expected him to be there, I would get worried, so frightened that he, too, was gone.

My father tried to reassure me in those moments, but also to strengthen me. I'll never forget something he said to me at a very young age: "Roma, remember that if you can bury your da, you can do anything. There won't be anything you can't do if you can bury your da." He knew that his death was my greatest fear. He also knew that day would come, and he wanted to strengthen me so that I would not fall apart in that moment, but be able to gather myself. To find the resources of strength within. And to know that he was by my side, always.

Unfortunately that day came sooner than I expected; my father died during my final year in drama school. In my deep grief, I was so worried that since his spirit had now gone from this earth, I would not be able to feel his love in the moon. That he would no longer be able to send messages. That I would see the moon and not feel his presence, as I always had before.

I was almost afraid to go outside and see.

But I finally walked out to the very backyard where he had

promised his moon messages. I looked up at the big, bright moon. And, sure enough, I felt him—his quiet love, so silent yet strong. I picked up his message: *Wherever you go in the world, Roma, the same moon will always be shining down on you. So never forget, no matter where you are, I will always be there, loving you.* Tears streamed down my face as I felt his love so powerfully.

The moon has been a beautiful comfort to me all these years. And I've now shared this message with my children. Even though we have the technology to be literally at each other's fingertips no matter how many miles may be between us, I sometimes text them when we are apart and say: *Go look at the moon! I left a message for you there.*

he will cover you with his feathers, and under his wings you will find refuge; his faithfulness will be your shield and rampart. PSALM 91:4

The moon, though it can shine so brightly, has no true light source of its own; it simply reflects the sun. I love the idea that when we send messages of love to the moon, the moon in return does what it does best . . . it reflects those messages to our loved ones. I like to imagine that the moonlight becomes love light.

Throughout the journey of my life, these symbols have helped me feel close to my parents despite their early deaths. Butterflies for my mother, the moon for my father. Both by extension have always reminded me that though I sometimes feel alone, they are still with me in spirit. And, of course, they remind me that I have another Father who has also never left my side: my Heavenly Father.

I've carried a longing for my parents in my heart for many years now. No matter how much I've grown, I still long for the touch of my mom's hand on my brow, the special cadence of her laugh, or my dad's quiet strength. I greatly miss their physical presence.

There are moments when I think it's just so sad and unfair that I haven't been able to share the joys of my life with my parents. I know without a doubt that the course of my career would have delighted my mother, who loved the theater. And I know both my parents would have adored meeting my beautiful daughter, Reilly; they would have been there for her birth and would have held their precious granddaughter in their arms and in their hearts. I know they would have loved meeting my husband, Mark, and the two fine sons, James and Cameron, whom he brought into my life. Of course I have missed my parents every single day since their deaths, but my faith allows me to believe that one day, all will be restored. Someday, there will be a heavenly reunion. Someday, I will see them again, and we will all walk hand in hand, like we did all those years ago.

For the truth is, we never walk alone.

You can do the impossible,
because you have been
through the unimaginable.

CHRISTINA RASMUSSEN

Remember

Remember me when I am gone away,
   Gone far away into the silent land;
   When you can no more hold me by the hand,
Nor I half turn to go yet turning stay.
Remember me when no more day by day
   You tell me of our future that you plann'd:
   Only remember me; you understand
It will be late to counsel then or pray.
Yet if you should forget me for a while
   And afterwards remember, do not grieve:
   For if the darkness and corruption leave
   A vestige of the thoughts that once I had,
Better by far you should forget and smile
   Than that you should remember and be sad.

Christina Georgina Rossetti

Death is nothing at all.

It does not count.

I have only slipped away into the next room.

Nothing has happened.

Everything remains exactly as it was.

I am I, and you are you,

and the old life that we lived so fondly together

is untouched, unchanged.

Whatever we were to each other, that we are still.

Call me by the old familiar name.

Speak of me in the easy way which you always used.

Put no difference into your tone.

Wear no forced air of solemnity or sorrow.

Laugh as we always laughed at the little jokes

that we enjoyed together.

Play, smile, think of me, pray for me.

Let my name be ever the household word that it always was.

Let it be spoken without an effort,

    without the ghost of a shadow upon it.

Life means all that it ever meant.

It is the same as it ever was.

There is absolute and unbroken continuity.

What is this death but a negligible accident?

Why should I be out of mind because I am out of sight?

I am but waiting for you, for an interval,

somewhere very near,

just round the corner.

All is well.

Nothing is hurt; nothing is lost.

One brief moment and all will be as it was before.

How we shall laugh at the trouble of parting

    when we meet again!

                 Henry Scott Holland

MY SURROGATE MOTHER

It is not flesh and blood, but heart which
makes us fathers and sons.

FRIEDRICH SCHILLER

I first met Della Reese on the set in Wilmington, North Carolina, where we were filming the pilot for *Touched by an Angel*. I had already gone through hair and makeup and even filmed a few scenes. But I was eager to meet this woman, this other angel who would be my counterpart on the show. As I wrapped a scene, I heard that Miss Della Reese had arrived and was getting made up. I went back to the makeup trailer to finally meet her—and there she was, wearing bright and colorful clothing that was nothing compared to the luminous smile she wore on her face. She *radiated* love and warmth and joy.

I walked up quietly, politely reaching out my hand and saying, "I just wanted to introduce myself."

Della stood up and said, "Oh, baby, I don't shake hands, I hug." And she wrapped me in the biggest, most loving embrace I had ever experienced.

It was love at first sight.

We are an unlikely duo when you think of it—a tough-talking black singer from Detroit, Michigan, and a small, soft-spoken white woman from Ireland. But we hit it off right away, talking about our lives, the challenges we had faced, and our strong faith, which we both knew kept us going and definitely brought us together on this project. The chemistry that we so easily shared offscreen was very present in our relationship on-screen, and I know it enhanced the experience for the viewers. Della, like Tess, was the older, wiser, tougher angel—feisty and formidable and fiercely protective of those she loves.

And in the protective way that Tess loved Monica, Della came to love me.

Now, deep within me, there lives a little girl still longing for a mother. Since the age of nearly eleven, I have been searching for that kind of tender, unconditional love that only a mother can give. And I found that in Della Reese.

Soon, we were always together on set. There is a lot of waiting between rehearsals and actual filming on a film set, so Della and I would meet in our trailers and play backgammon, share books, drink tea, and talk.

When my daughter, Reilly, was born, I chose Della to be her godmother, and at Reilly's christening, Della lifted my precious baby girl heavenward and said, "As long as there is breath in my body, I will always stand up for this child."

I can honestly say that there is absolutely no safer place in the world than in the arms of Della Reese.

Della and I share a love that is deeper than friendship. She became my family that very first day. I truly felt as if I had known her all my life. She has become the first person I call when I need wisdom, and she is a loving teacher and instructor.

A few years later, I was on the *Touched by an Angel* set in Salt Lake City, rehearsing the angel revelation scene, when I heard a commotion offstage. And then someone rushed up to me and said, "Roma, you must go see Della immediately. She needs you."

I quickly ran to Della's trailer, where I found her crying and incoherent, struggling to take off her angel costume and get changed into her regular clothes. I tried to calm her down and get a sense of what was going on. Della was clearly distraught and overwhelmed with grief. Something terrible had happened. "She's gone, she's gone," she cried out as she collapsed into my arms.

I managed to piece together that Della's only daughter had died.

I hardly knew what to do, but I did know that Della needed to get home to Los Angeles. I helped get her dressed and then we rushed into a waiting car to head to the Salt Lake City airport. As we were pulling away, I rolled down the window and called out to an assistant: "Please have someone grab my purse and some shoes and bring them to the airport!" I'd hardly even noticed that I was still in my white angel costume, with no shoes on my feet.

Della looked at me and said, "No, baby, you need to stay, Reilly needs you here." But I brushed aside her concern, now being the strong one in the relationship. "No, I'm coming with you," I said firmly.

Della looked at me sadly and took my hand in hers. "I don't want to talk," she said quietly as she turned to gaze out the window.

There is a holiness about your tears. Each one is a prayer that only God can understand.

KATHE WUNNENBURG

"That's okay," I said. "I won't say a word. I'll just be here with you the whole way, holding your hand."

When we got to the airport, I purchased tickets for the flight back to L.A. and met my assistant, Linda, who had brought me my purse, my ID, and a pair of shoes. We somehow made it through security and onto the plane without too much fuss. Della is such a recognizable person, but I knew that now was not the time to deal with requests for autographs. I was a guard dog, protecting my mama. No one would bother her. I would keep her safe until I got her home and into the loving arms of her husband, Franklin.

There was a moment during the flight when Della finally fell asleep, and I could feel the tension leave her body. I silently prayed that she could rest a bit before having to wake up and deal with the reality of this heartbreak. But after only a few moments, she jolted and awoke, and I could feel the remembering take place in her body. I squeezed her hand. My heart was breaking for her, and I silently prayed that God would give her strength and comfort.

When we arrived in L.A., I walked Della down the jetway to the gate, where Franklin was waiting. "Daddy," she said, which was what she called him, and she was enveloped in his embrace. I sat down in a nearby chair, wanting to give them privacy in this deep moment of grief, knowing that my job was done. I hadn't wanted her to be alone in her pain, and now she was with her beloved, and she could go home and begin the grieving process.

I didn't have anywhere to stay and hadn't packed anything for the trip, and I had planned to fly back home to Utah to be with my Reilly. But the last flight back had already left. I sat down, unsure what to do, and then I saw a familiar face. It was Martha Williamson, the executive producer of *Touched by an Angel*. She walked up to me and said, "Is it just you here by yourself?"

And I said, "Yes, Della has gone home with Franklin."

Martha smiled. "Well, I just had a feeling I needed to come and be here for one of my angels. I thought it was Della I came for. But now I guess I am here for you!" So I went home with her and flew back to Utah the next day.

A few months later, Della and I were back in Los Angeles, taking a walk on the beach together. Looking out on the beauty of the ocean, Della said, "God is wonderful, isn't He?" I nodded in agreement, grateful that she could still feel His goodness in this dark time in her life. "But really, baby," she continued, "I did not know until now just how wonderful He is. You see, He brought me into your life because you needed a mama, didn't He?" she said quietly. Again I nodded, now holding her hand as she gazed out at the grand expanse of the sea. "But, baby," she said softly, "I didn't know He was bringing you into my life because I was gonna need a baby girl . . ." Her voice caught with emotion, and I put my arms around her, tears rolling down my face as well. She wiped her eyes and turned to face me. "Will you be my baby girl, Roma?" she asked me.

"Yes," I said, my heart welling with emotion.

"Well," she said lovingly and with strength, "then I am your mama. I am your mama."

Now, in that moment, I was longing for my real mama and Della for her real baby girl. But we were also overflowing with gratitude to God for giving us each other to fill the holes in our aching hearts. God had a plan for us. We didn't know the comfort we would find from loving each other, but God knew.

The redemption of our losses doesn't make the pain go away; it doesn't mean the loss didn't happen. But it does mean that, in even the darkest moment, there can be light again.

The real hope is not in something we think we can do, but in God, who is making something good out of it in some way we cannot see.

THOMAS MERTON

There is an appointed time for everything.

And there is a time for every event under heaven.

A time to give birth, and a time to die;

A time to plant, and a time to uproot what is planted.

A time to kill, and a time to heal;

A time to tear down, and a time to build up.

A time to weep, and a time to laugh;

A time to mourn, and a time to dance.

A time to throw stones, and a time to gather stones;

A time to embrace, and a time to shun embracing.

A time to search, and a time to give up as lost;

A time to keep, and a time to throw away.

A time to tear apart, and a time to sew together;

A time to be silent, and a time to speak.

A time to love, and a time to hate;

A time for war, and a time for peace.

What profit is there to the worker from that in which he

toils?

I have seen the task which God has given

the sons of men with which to occupy themselves.

He has made everything appropriate in its time.

He has also set eternity in their heart,

yet so that man will not find out the work

which God has done from the beginning even to the end.

I know that there is nothing better for them

than to rejoice and to do good in one's lifetime;

moreover, that every man who eats and drinks

sees good in all his labor—it is the gift of God.

I know that everything God does will remain forever;

there is nothing to add to it and there is nothing

to take from it,

for God has so worked that men should fear Him.

That which is has been already

and that which will be has already been,

for God seeks what has passed by.

Ecclesiastes 3:1–15 (NASB)

Let me not pray to be sheltered from dangers
but to be fearless in facing them.

Let me not beg for the stilling of my pain
but for the heart to conquer it.

RABINDRANATH TAGORE

STRUGGLES MAKE YOU STRONGER

*Just when the caterpillar thought the world
was over, it became a butterfly.*

ENGLISH PROVERB

Mark and I had the privilege of bringing the epic story of Ben-Hur back to the big screen, a huge undertaking that involved lots of talented people, much travel, and a big crew for special effects.

But there is a small moment in the film, probably one that most people won't even notice, that has come to mean so much to me.

It comes toward the end of the film, as Judah Ben-Hur has just accomplished what he was striving to achieve for the entire film—revenge. He, along with his mother and sister, had been wrongfully imprisoned for the attempted assassination of the governor. He has just won the epic chariot race that led to the demise of his longtime nemesis, Messala. But as he stumbles out of the arena and looks around, he is surprised to find that instead of being filled with triumph from his victory, he feels profoundly empty. This driving force had been his mission for his entire life. Now, having achieved what he thought he so desperately needed, he realizes that his victory delivers no fulfillment.

As Judah begins to walk down the street, he sees a man being forced to carry a heavy wooden cross. The man is surrounded on either side by Roman guards, and Judah can see how deeply the man is suffering. Remembering his many years as a slave, forced to walk long distances with no water or rest, he rushes up to this poor man to offer some water. But the Romans kick him away. "No water for him!" they yell.

In anger, Judah grabs a rock to defend the man carrying the cross. But the man looks him in the eye and says: "I give my life of my own free will."

Judah stops in shock and watches the procession continue. He follows along silently as the group walks to the place where this man is crucified. Judah can't look away. As the man takes his last breaths, Judah hears Him say: "Father, forgive them, for they know not what they do."

The man on the cross is of course Jesus, and Judah is so overcome with emotion that he drops to his knees. He finally understands and knows what he needs to do. Revenge didn't quench his thirst. But forgiveness will.

Judah looks down at his hands. He's still clutching the rock that he grabbed back on the street to defend Jesus.

And as forgiveness fills his heart, he is able at last to let it go. The rock drops to the ground.

And he is finally free.

To me, that scene represents the need we all have to let go, to surrender. To hand our burdens over to God. Sometimes, like Judah, we don't realize how much we are carrying and how much it is weighing us down. Some-

Ring the bells that still can ring

Forget your perfect offering

There is a crack, a crack in everything

That's how the light gets in.

LEONARD COHEN

times we carry anger, like Judah. Other times, disappointment or sadness or regret. Usually the burden we carry stems from the struggles in our lives.

We all have the opportunity to kneel before God and lay our stuff down.

He will always take it.

And therein lies such freedom.

What is weighing you down? What loss have you experienced that you haven't been able to truly grieve or let go of?

Could you, like Judah, drop that rock and finally open your hands to receive what God wants to bestow?

God is always looking to redeem, restore, renew, and forgive.

Loss is a part of our lives, but it is in those times of darkness that God forges a new person. Just as the caterpillar must go into the darkness of the cocoon to become a butterfly, we often find that God's loving redemption is strongest in our most painful suffering. God is always looking for ways to transform us through our circumstances if we will just let Him in. We must remember that through the struggle, God is building our wings so that we can soon emerge a new creation, stronger than before, and able to fly.

God is the ultimate creator and miracle worker. He can make anything from our lives—no matter what they look like. He can make beauty from ashes, winged creatures from creepy crawlies, light from dark, life from death. It is when we stop and listen for Him, for grace, that we can remember the truth, that we can reframe what is happening. Though the facts remain the same, a simple reframing of the story can change the ultimate experience, and of course the ending. Then I can see the truth: I have not fallen into a deep dark pit that I cannot get out of. Rather, this darkness is forging my new being.

For there in the journey and stuck in the sting, the struggle . . . the struggle . . . is what gives you wings!

KAREN KINGSBURY

If I have learned anything, I know this to be true: there is no growth without pain.

The very things we struggle with actually give us the strength and character to become who we are. Think about the fact that the butterfly begins as such an ordinary bug. But then it becomes a stunning creature that can fly great distances. Did you know that monarch butterflies can fly up to three thousand miles during their migration? That they can fly at speeds up to twenty miles per hour? Some pilots have actually seen them at an altitude of eleven thousand feet. The beauty and strength of a simple butterfly remind me that with God all things are possible.

You can choose to stay a caterpillar, crawling on the ground your entire life. Or you can subject yourself to the transformation process, the pain of metamorphosis, and become someone who, with God's help, can fly to the highest heights, move at great speeds, and explore the world with wonder and gratitude.

*I consider that the sufferings of this
present time are not worth comparing
with the glory about to be revealed to us.*

ROMANS 8:18 (NRSV)

For Courage

When the light around you lessens
And your thoughts darken until
Your body feels fear turn
Cold as a stone inside,

When you find yourself bereft
Of any belief in yourself
And all you unknowingly
Leaned on has fallen,

When one voice commands
Your whole heart,
And it is raven dark,

Steady yourself and see
That it is your own thinking
That darkens your world,

Search and you will find
A diamond-thought of light,

Know that you are not alone
And that this darkness has purpose;

Gradually it will school your eyes
To find the one gift your life requires
Hidden within this night-corner.

Invoke the learning
Of every suffering
You have suffered.

Close your eyes.
Gather all the kindling
About your heart
To create one spark.
That is all you need
To nourish the flame
That will cleanse the dark
Of its weight of festered fear.

A new confidence will come alive
To urge you towards higher ground
Where your imagination
Will learn to engage difficulty
As its most rewarding threshold!

John O'Donohue

Japanese Bowl

I'm like one of those Japanese bowls
That were made long ago
I have some cracks in me
They have been filled with gold

That's what they used back then
When they had a bowl to mend
It did not hide the cracks

It made them shine instead
So now every old scar shows
From every time I broke
And anyone's eyes can see
I'm not what I used to be
But in a collector's mind
All of these jagged lines
Make me more beautiful
And worth a much higher price
I'm like one of those Japanese bowls
I was made long ago
I have some cracks you can see
See how they shine of gold

Peter Mayer

Thank you, God.
That though our hearts break
in this world,
You are always there.
Thank you, that during my
darkest moments,
You were carrying me.
Even as I felt so alone.
May I hold fast to the
hope that you provide,
that you can raise the dead,
that in the dark, light is coming,
that ultimately, all
brokenness will be healed,
relationship restored,
that wholeness and peace
is our birthright.

Like it or not, we either add to the darkness of indifference and out-and-out evil which surrounds us or we light a candle to see by.

MADELEINE L'ENGLE

It is better to light one candle than to curse the darkness.

AUTHOR UNKNOWN

KINDNESS

two

KINDNESS

No one is born hating another person because
of the color of his skin, or his background, or his religion.
People must learn to hate, and if they can learn to hate,
they can be taught to love, for love comes more naturally
to the human heart than its opposite.

NELSON MANDELA

I WAS BORN in Derry City, Northern Ireland, a beautiful border town in the North West of Ireland. Yet throughout my childhood, my town was filled with tension and violence that began when I was about eight years old. I grew up in the midst of a war that became known in Ireland as "the Troubles."

Ours was a story of neighboring people wanting different things and being unable to find common ground. The Catholics desired independence from the United Kingdom, hoping to become part of the Republic of Ireland (Republicans); while the Protestants wanted to remain a part of the

United Kingdom (Loyalists). Both sides harbored animosity, distrust, and prejudice toward each other.

When the violence between the communities began to escalate, the British army arrived. But before long, it became clear that those sent in to establish peace became an army of occupation, and the conflict only increased with their presence.

As children, we would sometimes get detoured on our way home from school because of bomb scares or gun battles. We learned from an early age to hide behind cars and walls, quickly becoming little experts on telling how close the gunfire was. If it was a loud crack, you better take cover quickly; if it was more muted, you were probably safe for the moment and could continue on your way home.

We lived on the same street as John and Pat Hume. John was one of the great politicians of the day and was instrumental in bringing peace to Northern Ireland, and went on to win the Nobel Peace Prize. My mother and Pat became great friends, and their young daughter Mo was named after my mother.

Not long after my beloved mom passed away, I went to the cemetery to put flowers on her grave for Mother's Day. It was chilly and damp, and the wind blew sharply on the hillside where she was buried. I had bundled up in my favorite red woolen cape, with fake fur trim, to protect me from the sharp chill in the air. I was with my Auntie Ruby, my mother's only sister, and we brought with us some beautiful pansies, my mother's favorite flower.

The Town I Loved So Well

But when I returned how my eyes have burned

To see how a town could be brought to its knees

By the armoured cars and the bombed-out bars

And the gas that hangs on to every breeze.

Now the army's installed by the old gasyard wall

And the damned barbed wire gets higher and higher

With their tanks and their guns, oh my God,

what have they done

To the town I loved so well.

Phil Coulter

My eyes were filled with tears as I placed this small offering by her tombstone. Her absence in my life had broken my heart, and as we stood by her graveside, I missed her so desperately I could hardly breathe. I longed to hear her laughter and the sound of her voice calling my name. I ached to feel the warmth and safety of her arms around me. I didn't know if my mother could see me, if she could see the flowers I had so carefully selected for her. I longed to have her back.

My auntie's hand was on my shoulder when we heard the first loud gunshot. We both dropped to the ground instinctively, but this area of the cemetery offered no protection.

A wide, lonely hillside on a cold afternoon. And here I was, wearing a bright red cape.

My aunt pulled me to my feet and we began to run to see if we could find a large gravestone to duck behind. The shots rang out, and we saw a few others running for cover in the area around us.

"Get down, get down where you are!" a man yelled at us, seeing my bright red cape and realizing how much of a target it made me.

My aunt pulled me to the ground, just as we both smelled a scent like burned hair. She covered me with her body as we lay on the cold, wet earth, praying for protection and hoping that the battle would end.

Finally, the shooting stopped, and after we were certain it was over, we cautiously picked ourselves up off the ground and embraced in gratitude. Then, with my hand tight in hers, Auntie Ruby hurried me down the hill toward the safety of home.

As soon as we opened the front door, I ran to our kitchen, tears streaming down my face, to find my dad.

He held me close as my aunt told him what had happened.

He rubbed my back, calming me down. But then he grabbed the hood of my cape and said, "Ruby, come look at this."

And there, on the fake fur trim of my hooded red cape, was a large singed hole where a bullet had narrowly missed my head.

"Oh, thanks be to God," gasped my aunt as my father nodded. "Yes, thanks be to God indeed."

Years later, when Della heard that story, she said, "There were angels watching over you that day, baby." That is for sure.

Growing up in such troubled times planted in me the desire to work toward creating peace in the world.

The River Foyle divides Derry; and as the Troubles escalated, the communities on either side of the river became more and more segregated. It broke my heart to see our town split in two. So much anger and fear and sadness and loss on both sides. But my dad refused to give up hope. He always looked

You've got to be taught to hate and fear,
You've got to be taught from year to year,
It's got to be drummed in your dear little ear
You've got to be carefully taught!
You've got to be taught to be afraid
Of people whose eyes are oddly made,
And people whose skin is a different shade
You've got to be carefully taught.
You've got to be taught before it's too late,
Before you are six or seven or eight,
To hate all the people your relatives hate
You've got to be carefully taught!

RICHARD RODGERS AND OSCAR HAMMERSTEIN II

for ways to build bridges. He always spoke of tolerance and love. He taught me that we should reach out to each other in neighborly love and support.

In those years, I listened to the music of Simon and Garfunkel and replayed their cassette over and over. They sang of a bridge over troubled water. Clearly we needed that in our community—and indeed we would rejoice to finally see a new Peace Bridge opened over the River Foyle in 2011. But back in the 1970s, my dad encouraged me to explore how we each could be that bridge in our own lives. How we could be angels of peace in the lives of others if only we were willing to let God use us. My dad reminded me that we just needed to have the eyes to see the opportunities and the openness of heart to see each calling to love. He taught me to pray and to ask God for His guidance in my life.

I always remember my father saying, "Love is a verb." Quiet by nature, he was more prone to performing small acts of kindness than peppering you with words of adoration. He was a thoughtful man, and I adored him. After my mother's death, I became more attached to him than ever. He was a schoolmaster, and later ran a mortgage-loan company; and in our predominantly working-class neighborhood, he was very well respected—not just because he had a college education and wore a shirt and tie every day but because he was never condescending to people. He was respectful and kind; and even though people in our community called each other by their first names, my dad remained Mr. Downey to many.

He volunteered to teach grown men in our community to read and write, yet did this discreetly to allow these men their pride and privacy. He was always seeking to help the world in little ways. And his acts of kindness spread far and wide.

His example has been an inspiration to me my entire life. It has caused me to commit to treating people with kindness and respect and to be on the lookout for ways to brighten someone's day. It's easy to get busy and forget to share simple kindnesses, but I know from experience that little acts of compassion add up to a life of great significance.

I've learned that people will forget what you said, people will forget what you did, but people will never forget how you made them feel.

MAYA ANGELOU

Do all the good you can,

By all the means you can,

In all the ways you can,

In all the places you can,

At all the times you can,

To all the people you can,

As long as you ever can.

John Wesley

THE FLANNEL SHEETS

Actions speak louder than words . . .

MARK TWAIN

I was eighteen when I finally left Derry. As the Troubles continued with no sign of letting up, my dad knew an education would be my passport to a new and bigger life. So, with his blessing, when I graduated from high school I first went to Brighton College of Art, in the South of England, and then on to London and drama school. In London, I rented a room in one of those big Georgian houses that had been converted into flats. I missed my dad and went back to visit as often as I could.

It was late in the spring of my last semester in drama school, and I was planning a trip home to Ireland to stay with my father for the unexpected ordination of my eldest half brother, John. John was many years older than me, and had felt the calling to the priesthood late in his life, so it was a surprise for all of us. I knew how proud my father was that his oldest son was going to become a priest.

In the absence of cell phones, the lodgers in my flat shared a black pay phone in the chilly hallway by the front door. As I telephoned my father to confirm my travel arrangements the day before my flight, I pictured my small town and the grand celebration I knew was being planned. When I heard my father's voice on the other end of the line, a feeling of safety immediately washed over me. The sweet sound of his lilting voice was so comforting and familiar, even over the phone. We discussed my early flight the next morning from Heathrow Airport to Belfast, how I would be picked up at the airport and that I would be home in time for tea.

As we wrapped up our call, my father, a man of few words, said that he was so glad I was coming home and that, because of the ever-present dampness in our Derry air, he had hung my favorite yellow flannel sheets on the indoor line to air.

Our climate in the North of Ireland is damp at the best of times. To this day, when it rains in Malibu, I affectionately call it a "Derry Day." This was a time before dryers, and we just had a washtub and a wringer to do the laundry. In Ireland, we were rarely able to dry anything outside due to the rainy weather, so people in our town had indoor clotheslines, usually in the kitchen where there might be a stove to provide warmth and dryness.

I went to bed that night imagining the soft, cozy feel of those flannel sheets, prepared for me by my loving father. My little suitcase, packed for the trip and slightly frayed, was standing ready at the end of the bed.

In the middle of the night the guy from the front flat

began pounding on my door. "Wake up, Irish!" he yelled. "And tell your bloody family not to call in the middle of the night!" My heart skipped a beat as I rushed out of bed, fear flooding every step down the cold hallway in the dark. I lifted the heavy receiver, delaying a moment longer before I finally whispered hello.

My brother Lawrence was on the phone. My dad was dead. Lawrence told me it was sudden; apparently Dad's heart gave out.

I did not know what to do. I must have said something. I must have hung up the telephone. I know I slid down the wall and sat in the dark. I'm not sure for how long. I was in shock. I had just heard his voice. I had just spoken to him. How could he be gone? How had the very thing I feared most since my mother's death really happened?

I remembered how my dad had always said, "If you can bury your da, you can do anything." I knew I was no longer a little girl. I was making my way in the world, and I knew how proud my father was of my life in London, my dream of being an actress. But I still wanted him here. I didn't want to have to bury him.

I knew I could not sleep, so I went back to my room and waited until the sun came up. Then I took the flight I was scheduled to take, but now my journey home had a whole new, unwelcome purpose.

By the time I got to Derry, my father's body had already been returned to our brick row house for the wake, our front door displaying the black bow of mourning. In our loving Irish tradition, we still lay out our dead in our living rooms for the great parade of friends and family and neighbors, coming to pay their respects. The Irish wake is designed to provide the family with love and support as they send off their loved ones and say good-bye.

I walked into our dark little hallway and past the room where he lay. I was not ready yet to see him dead, needing first the courage that comes only from a cup of tea. Tea, the Irish solution to everything. So I slipped into our kitchen, so familiar to me in every way, and a vision took my breath away. For there, hanging on the indoor clothesline to air, were my favorite yellow flannel sheets, the last loving act of a most thoughtful man. I held them to my face, breathed in their kindness, and cried.

John walked into the room and saw me standing, holding the sheets. Not knowing of the last conversation I had with my father, he was focused on the practical, the fact that we would soon have countless friends and family streaming through the door to pay their respects. "Oh, we have to get these old sheets down before people come calling," he said as he went to put the teakettle on.

"Oh, not yet, not yet," I said quietly. I wanted those sheets there while I had my cup of tea, one final reminder of the kindness of my father, of how, during his last moments on earth, he was thinking of me, his youngest daughter, and how he could best welcome me home.

If I speak in the
tongues of men and
of angels but have not
love, I am a noisy gong or
a clanging cymbal. And if
I have prophetic powers and
understand all mysteries and all
knowledge, and if I have all faith, so as
to remove mountains, but have not love, I am
nothing. If I give away all I have, and if I deliver up
my body to be burned, but have not love, I gain nothing.

Love is patient and kind; love does not envy or boast;
it is not arrogant or rude. It does not insist on its own
way; it is not irritable or resentful; it does not rejoice at
wrongdoing, but rejoices with the truth. Love bears all
things, believes all things, hopes all things, endures all
things. Love never ends As for prophecies, they will pass
away; as for tongues, they will cease; as for knowledge,
it will pass away. For we know in part and we prophesy
in part, but when the perfect comes, the partial will pass
away. When I was a child, I spoke like a child, I thought
like a child, I reasoned like a child. When I became a man,
I gave up childish ways. For now we see in a mirror dimly,
but then face-to-face. Now I know in part; then I shall
know fully, even as I have been fully known.

So now faith, hope, and love abide, these three; but the
greatest of these is love.

1 Corinthians 13 (ESV)

Lord,

make me an instrument
of Your peace.
Where there is hatred,
let me sow love;
where there is injury, pardon; where
there is doubt, faith;
where there is despair, hope;
where there is darkness, light; where
there is sadness, joy.
O, Divine Master,
grant that I may not so much seek
to be consoled as to console;
to be understood as to understand;
to be loved as to love;
for it is in giving that we receive;
it is in pardoning that we are
pardoned; it is in dying that we are
born again to eternal life.

PRAYER OF SAINT FRANCIS

Do not think that love, in order to be genuine,
has to be extraordinary. What we need is to love
without getting tired.

How does a lamp burn?
Through the continuous input of small drops of oil.
If the drops of oil run out, the light of the lamp will cease, and
the bridegroom will say, "I do not know you." (Matthew 25:12).

My daughters, what are these drops of oil in our lamps? They
are the small things of daily life: faithfulness, punctuality, small
words of kindness, a thought for others, our way of being silent,
of looking, of speaking, and of acting. These are the true drops
of love . . .

   Be faithful in small things, because it is in them that your
strength lies.

Mother Teresa

WHAT IS A SMILE WORTH?

If you want to lift yourself up, lift up someone else.

BOOKER T. WASHINGTON

Many years ago, on the very first season of *Touched by an Angel*, we shot an episode that featured the organization Operation Smile. Operation Smile was founded to provide a safe, simple surgery to the countless impoverished children who are born with a craniofacial anomaly, usually a cleft palate or lip. This is a common issue, occurring in one out of every 500 to 750 births. Doctors can repair the lip or palate easily, and usually do so in the United States by the time the child is three months old for a cleft lip, or by the time the child is between twelve and eighteen months old for a cleft palate. Yet across the rest of the globe, many of these children do not have access to this straightforward, forty-five-minute surgery.

It was a powerful episode to film for both the cast and crew, and viewers across the world were touched deeply as well. I soon became actively involved in the organization as a spokesperson and began to travel around the globe, helping them on their mission to change the world one smile at a time.

Many of these children are born into cultures where stigmas are attached to such an anomaly, where it is viewed as a curse and a shame on the family, with no hope of a cure. Some children with cleft lips and palates cannot eat properly or smile or speak. The mothers of these children worry. They worry that their children will never have a normal life. The worry they will die. They pray for a cure, not realizing that one exists.

And then they hear rumors about this medical group coming, a group of doctors who supposedly have the ability to fix faces. And a seed of hope is planted. This seed of hope drives these women to walk miles or get on a bus to go to far-off places, all in hopes that their child might be chosen and given a chance at a normal life.

They arrive and see our faces and our smiles and our brochures with pictures that promise a fix, a solution to the problem that has plagued their beloved child since birth. And so they hand their babies over. They hand them over to strangers who don't even speak their language. Talk about a lesson in trust. They trust that with Operation Smile, there is a chance.

My favorite moment in every mission is when, forty-five minutes after a mother has handed over her baby to outsiders, she sees us emerge from surgery and give that baby back to her. It is like a rebirth. The child, whom that mother thought would never get to smile, smiles up at her for the first time. She is shrouded in joy and gratitude, tears stream down her face, and we all rejoice together in the power of healing, in the gift of second chances.

The first time I had the chance to give a healed child back to his mother, I was crying just as much as the mother. I looked at the child I held in my arms. His beautiful little face had been perfectly repaired, and I carefully carried him out to where his mother stood, alone and silent. She had been praying, fear and hope battling in her watchful gaze. Her face brightened

The only way you can serve God is by serving other people.

RICK WARREN

when she saw us walk toward her, and her eyes quickly found her child's face. There was her little son, perfectly restored. And she cried, this time tears of relief. Now her child would have a normal life.

It was one of the most amazing moments of my life, second only to the birth of my own little girl. To be the one to hand back a restored child to its mother, to see this mother's greatest prayer answered, felt like being one of God's angels.

And I've learned that the operation doesn't just change the life of that little boy or girl or mother. But when they travel back to their villages and the villagers see this little child restored, it creates a ripple of hope for the whole community. Because if that little baby's dreams can come true, maybe it can happen to them. Maybe taking a risk or taking a journey to see what might be out there could be the beginning of a new life.

I can't even begin to describe how powerful it is to see hope renewed in a person's life. When I go on these missions, of course I want to "help" people; but really, I do it selfishly, too. Because I, too, am transformed. To see the doctors and nurses who are volunteering their time to make these dreams come true fills me with a sense of hope and possibility. They are the angels. I watch as they train local doctors to perform these surgeries, so that after they are gone, hope will remain. Watching them reminds me of the gifts we all have to share with the world. As the old Chinese proverb says, "Give a man a fish, and he will eat for a day; teach a man to fish, and he will eat for a lifetime." When I witness the courage and trust that God instills in these mothers—the trust to bring their babies to these doctors—I am reminded of the goodness of God and how He truly performs miracles through His children every day if we are willing.

I love the founders of the Operation Smile organization, Dr. Bill Magee and his wife, Kathy. I am grateful to them for their example and their friendship. They possessed the empathic eyes to see the great need for this organization, the brave heart to see the possibilities, and the faith to try to help. "If we don't take care of that child, there's no guarantee that anyone else will," Kathy says.

What if they had just shrugged their shoulders and said "Oh, how sad" but did nothing? What if they had waited for others to step up?

But they didn't. They knew that God calls all of us to care for one another.

We sometimes think we have to do huge things to change the world. We don't. We just have to have the eyes to see the needs around us and to use the capabilities God has given us to help in small ways. God is waiting for us to be his hands in this world.

We should be shining lamps,
giving light to all around us.

CATHERINE McCAULEY

When I was a boy and I would see
scary things in the news,
my mother would say to me,
"Look for the helpers. You will always find
people who are helping."

FRED ROGERS

How wonderful it is that
nobody need wait a single moment
before starting to improve the world.

ANNE FRANK

AN UNEXPECTED ANGEL

*You can preach a better sermon with your life
than with your lips.*

OLIVER GOLDSMITH

For almost ten years, I was able to deliver a message of
faith, hope, and love on network television. More than
twenty million people tuned in each week to hear the message "God loves you." We would take them on a journey and
remind them that they are never truly alone. Because of that
message, when people ran into me on the street, they didn't
necessarily ask for an autograph. I wasn't just an actress they
admired. I was an angel. They wanted a hug.

When you play an angel on TV, people begin to think
you are an angel in real life. Sometimes when people met
me, they spoke quietly and reverently, as if they were in
the presence of someone holy! Now, I am the first person
to tell you that I am just as flawed as everyone else, that I
am far from perfect. But playing an angel for almost ten
years not only had a positive influence on the audience,

it had a huge impact on me as well. I began to realize that we all have the opportunity to be an angel if we are just willing to show kindness and grace and love to those around us.

For the almost ten years that I lived in Salt Lake City, I often went to Primary Children's Hospital to visit the children who were sick. The people of Salt Lake City treated us very well for the entire ten years that we filmed there. They took pride in what we were doing and embraced us like family wherever we went. I had gotten into the habit of stopping by the hospital when I could to provide a moment of joy for the many families who had sick children, and I would often visit the tiny babies in the NICU. If the parents weren't there, I would sometimes take a Polaroid of me visiting their baby and leave it on the incubator with a note saying that an angel had visited while they were gone. Over the years, I met many of these children in the neighborhoods where we filmed. A mom would show up with a now robust toddler to thank me and tell me that my visit had given them hope at a stressful time in their lives.

One day, around Christmas, I was at the hospital. I was wearing a Santa hat as a way to bring a festive spirit to the families who were sequestered in those halls. As I walked down the corridor, excited to see the next patient, I saw a family exiting one of the rooms. I quickly pulled off my hat and backed into a corner. There was no question what this family had just experienced. You could feel the grief gust like a wind out of this room. But the mother looked up, saw me, and gasped. She rushed over, saying, "Monica, here you are!" She grabbed my hands and said, "Oh, Monica, I prayed that an angel would come for my baby. And here you are! Here you are."

I stiffened, not knowing what to say. My heart ached for her.

Monica was the name of the angel I played on television, but *I* wasn't Monica, I was just Roma. I wasn't an angel; I was just a normal human being. I did not know what to say. This grieving woman had enveloped me in a hug, and she had just experienced the worst thing a parent can experience. So I just held her; I wrapped my arms around her and prayed quietly with her. I prayed with all my heart.

After a few moments, she pulled back and looked me in the eyes, tears still streaming down her cheeks. "Thank you," she said quietly, "that was just what I needed." And then she returned to her husband and family, still huddled just outside the room, and they all walked down the hospital corridor.

I stood there, my heart beating fast, overwhelmed with emotion, but also questioning whether I had been dishonest. That woman wanted and needed an angel, and all she got was me. But I also saw the comfort that my presence had provided. If I could make her smile through her tears, maybe I had done the right thing. If I had made her believe in God's faithfulness, perhaps everything was okay.

When I got home that evening, I sat down and called Della to tell her the story. "Oh, Della, I didn't know what to say. I was afraid to appear to be something I'm not. I should have said something, but I could not find the words."

Della laughed. "Baby, I don't understand what you're so upset about."

I tried to explain again. "But Della, she thought that God had sent an angel to her."

To which Della said, "And who said He didn't?" She paused. "That woman didn't need an actress, baby. She needed an angel. And if we are going to be used in this series for His highest good, then we need to learn to get out of the way."

As I hung up the phone that evening, I prayed, thanking God both for using me and for Della, who as always possessed the wisdom I desperately needed. Who was I to say God wasn't using me in that moment? How many other times had I limited Him and not been available to be a light to someone who needed it?

That moment has stuck with me through the years. And I've tried to be attuned to the ways that a simple act of kindness on my part might be the very thing a person needs, the very thing to remind them that they are not alone. The dictionary defines "angel" as "a spiritual being that serves especially as a messenger from God." We are all spiritual beings, and we all have the ability to be messengers of God. I know Della has been an angel for me, as has my own precious daughter, Reilly. My husband has been an angel for me more times that I can count, and for our boys. I pray that I will be an angel to others, every day. We are all here together—during the good times and the bad, the ups and downs—and sometimes we need a hand to pull us up, and at other times we have the strength to reach down and encourage someone else. That is what the family of God is here to do—keep walking forward, eyes heavenward, as we do the work of our maker.

In that moment, when that grieving woman probably felt so heartbroken and alone, God used me to remind her . . . *I'm here with you, I'm always here. Trust in me.*

Trust in me.

In my books, and sometimes even in real life, I have it in me at my best to be a saint to other people, and by saint I mean life-giver, someone who is able to bear to others something of the Holy Spirit, whom the creeds describe as the Lord and Giver of Life. Sometimes, by the grace of God, I have it in me to be Christ to other people. And so, of course, have we all—the life-giving, life-saving, and healing power to be saints, to be Christs, maybe at rare moments even to ourselves.

FREDERICK BUECHNER

Loaves and Fishes

This is not
the age of information.

This is *not*
the age of information.

Forget the news,
and the radio,
and the blurred screen.

This is the time
of loaves
and fishes.

People are hungry,
and one good word is bread
for a thousand.

David Whyte

Lord, may I be reminded
of your presence in my life,
may I have the eyes to see
the needs of your people,
may I have a heart to
feel them
and the willingness to see how
I might help.
May I see each of your children
as my own,
and seek only to be a
bringer of light.
May people see me and be inspired
by the goodness in the world.
May kindness be my mantle
and my sword.

I learned that courage was not the absence of fear, but the triumph over it. The brave man is not he who does not feel afraid, but he who conquers that fear.

NELSON MANDELA

The Lord is my light and my salvation—
whom shall I fear?
The Lord is the stronghold of my life—
of whom shall I be afraid?

PSALM 27:1 (NIV)

COURAGE

three

COURAGE

*Promise me you'll always remember: You're braver than you
believe, and stronger than you seem,
and smarter than you think.*

WINNIE THE POOH (A. A. MILNE)

THE WORD "en*courage*" means to embolden one with *courage*, and I'm so thankful for the many people in my life who have emboldened me, urging me to go after my dreams. It began with my mother and her loving enthusiasm, signing me up for dance and music classes, and her quiet, loving support from the back of the room at all those lessons. It continued with my father, who pushed me to pursue an education and who always told me I was strong, capable, and smart.

But they weren't the only ones who planted the seeds of courage and confidence in me.

By the time I graduated from art school in Brighton, I knew I wanted to be a professional actor. I had studied the work of the Dutch artist Vincent van Gogh, and he had said a curious thing in one of his many letters to his brother Theo. Growing dissatisfied with his work, he expressed that he no longer wanted to be the painter but rather he wanted to be the paint.

When I read this, I instantly understood it in some unspoken way. I wanted to become the "paint" in my work, too. To breathe life into a script, to become a character, to tell a story. I wanted to be an actor. I realized my dream was to be onstage. I decided the best way to achieve this was to further my studies at the Drama Studio in London. I interviewed twice and was finally offered a place at this prestigious school. I was thrilled and so excited about the quality of training I would receive, but my heart sank when I was turned down for a grant to cover the cost of the tuition. I knew I couldn't afford it on my own and was trying to process my disappointment when a miracle occurred.

Three extraordinary people who I had been working with on a summer theater project banded together and offered to put up the money for me to attend. They told me they believed in me and wanted to invest in my future. It wasn't a loan, they assured me, it was an investment in me. They didn't want me to have to turn down this wonderful opportunity. The only thing they asked was that I pay the kindness forward with my life. And I have tried to do that over the years to honor their generosity.

I had never experienced such unbelievable, unselfish kindness before. But before I could accept, I told them I had to talk it over with my father. My dad was stunned. Of course he wished he had enough money to pay the tuition himself, but it was more than our family could afford. Knowing this was an incredible opportunity for me, he said he couldn't let pride stand in the way, and he gave me permission to accept.

These three wonderful angels gave me so much more than just the tuition fees. They gave me encouragement and confidence. They stepped up and showed that they believed in me, a belief that made all the difference. It made me want to work as hard as I possibly could to show them their investment in me was worthwhile. I didn't want to let them down.

The agreement was that they would cover the tuition, but I needed to get a job to cover my rent and living expenses. I wasn't afraid of hard work, and I immediately got a job as a waitress so I could cover my costs.

I excelled in my studies in London, and even went on to win the highest award the school offered: "Most Promising Student of the Year." Then, just one month before graduation, my father died. I was devastated. Not having him with me at the pivotal moment of accepting my diploma broke my heart. I wanted to see his eyes shining with pride as I walked across the stage, his heart bursting with the knowledge that my whole life was still in front of me, beckoning.

So here I was, finally out of school, and my beloved parents had both passed on and my childhood home in Northern Ireland had been sold. I was trained and ready and eager to start my professional life. Some of my friends in the program were planning to move to New York after graduation. I began to wonder if I could take that leap of faith as well. I was a young woman with a big dream, and I knew that the journey of a thousand miles begins with the first step.

I was scared, of course. The unknown opened up before me. But when nothing is certain, everything is possible. I prayed I would know what direction to take, that I would be guided to each next step, and that I would have the courage to take it.

Looking back, I can see that if my father had still been alive, I might never have considered moving to America. But I was young and filled with a sense of adventure. So I packed my bags and joined the ranks of thousands of young actors and actresses who pour into New York City each year. I came looking for the American dream.

I remember those early years of walking all over the city in search of a job. I often didn't have the fare for a taxi, so it was walking or buses or the subway, uptown and downtown and crosstown, to readings and meetings, sometimes several a day. I came home each night hoping to see the light on the answering machine flashing with the offer of a job. But it rarely flashed, and I frequently felt tremendously insecure.

To be an actor, you have to learn to live with fear.

Even if you're on the right track, you'll get run over if you just sit there.

WILL ROGERS

Every actor, no matter how good, no matter how seasoned, must face the fear that inevitably arises when you walk onto a stage in front of hundreds of people. Rosalind Russell, the American actress from the 1940s and '50s, once said, "Acting is standing up naked and turning around very slowly." Of course, she was speaking about being emotionally naked, about appearing vulnerable in front of others.

Actors have to learn to live with the fear of being vulnerable, and to conquer it.

I knew that in order to survive pursuing acting as a career, I had to develop a thick skin and the drive to keep going in the face of rejection. This was hard for me, as I am naturally tenderhearted and sensitive, but I knew that thick skin would provide an armor that would protect me. I had to learn not to take the setbacks to heart and not to take rejection personally.

You never know how strong you are until being strong is your only choice.

BOB MARLEY

There are often hundreds of actors pursuing just a few roles on each show. And the truth is that you could give the audition of your life, and they still might reject you just because of the color of your hair or because you are too short or too tall or too different from how directors envision the character.

Even though you know the rejection isn't personal, it often feels personal, and it hurts. That's when the thick skin is necessary.

But I had to learn to separate from the rejection. *It doesn't define who I am. The rejection isn't rejection of me. Acting is what I do, but it's not who I am.*

You can imagine that in those early days, before I had learned to disassociate, I struggled. I can see now that there was still within me a little child who felt the loss of her mother and a painful sense of abandonment. Rejections reopened old wounds that her death had created. And as these hurts reemerged, I no longer had my father there to offer his quiet words of encouragement and compassion.

Courage is resistance to fear, mastery of fear, not absence of fear.

MARK TWAIN

No matter what your profession, we all face those feelings sometimes. Feelings of unworthiness. Feelings of failure. Feelings of defeat.

But we don't have to stay in those places. I have found that the best remedy to negative self-talk is to try to move myself from a place of fear into a space of love. I start by simply thinking about the people I love. Remember Julie Andrews in *The Sound of Music* encouraging the von Trapp children to think of a few of their favorite things when they were afraid of the storm? Well, that's a version of what I do. I count my blessings, I pray, and I connect to God. Then I am reminded that God has a plan for my life, even when I do not always see it myself.

The time spent in that space of love restores me and gives me courage and joy, and my sense of purpose rises again. I am filled back up to go out into the world and chase my dreams, energized, excited, and full of faith.

A journey of a thousand miles must begin with a single step.

LAO TZU

I spent several years in New York trying to make things happen. I booked some regional theater shows, which were good experiences but did not pay much. In between shows, I went to acting classes and voice classes and exercise classes, making sure that I was ready. An acting teacher of mine always said that if opportunity knocks, it needs to find you ready and prepared, not taking a nap on the couch. You've got to stay well tuned in your craft.

During my years in Manhattan, I had the good fortune to meet all sorts of wonderful people who respected the struggle of the aspiring actors who populate the city and would do their part to cheer them up. The first celebrity I ever met came up to me one night when I was working as a coat-check girl in a fancy Upper West Side restaurant. It was seasonal work, but on a cold winter night I could pull in some decent tips, making anywhere from twenty-five cents to a dollar per coat. I would arrive at five o'clock to get set up for the night, and most customers would arrive between seven and eight. I would check people's coats, sit and read for a few hours while they dined, and then retrieve their coats for them around ten or eleven. One night, Regis Philbin walked up and asked me what I was reading. I looked up and recognized his face immediately. I told him the title of my book, and he looked at me with that famous twinkle in his eye, and said, "Oh, do I detect a bit of an accent?"

I laughed and said, "Yes, I'm from Ireland."

We chatted for a bit, and then he went off to enjoy dinner with his lovely wife, Joy. He left me a twenty-dollar tip, and I will never forget his kindness.

Many years later, when I was doing publicity in New York City for *Touched by an Angel*, I went on his show with Kathie Lee Gifford, and I told him the story. Regis laughed at the end of it and pretended to wipe his brow. "Phew! I was worried for a bit that I had stiffed you!"

We soon became friends, and many years later Mark and I hosted a birthday luncheon for Regis and Joy at our Malibu home. Kathie Lee and I became very dear friends as well. She did a few guest appearances on *Touched by an Angel*, and I was honored to work with her as an actress. Kathie Lee is a talented, strong woman of faith and is just lovely to be around.

My coat checking soon gave way to some acting work, and I was finally cast Off Broadway, at New York's Public Theater and the Roundabout Theatre, doing Shaw and Ibsen and Shakespeare, wonderful roles in classical plays. I was thrilled to be finally doing what I was trained for and what I loved. It wasn't Broadway yet, but it was interesting, quality work, and it paid, supplementing my other part-time gigs. And then one evening at intermission, the stage manager popped into my room and said, "We have a special guest who wants to meet you."

Sir Rex Harrison had been in the audience, and he walked into my dressing room in his impeccably tailored suit. I practically fainted. It was such an honor to meet this movie star, most beloved for his role as Henry Higgins in *My Fair Lady*.

Sir Rex was mounting a production of W. Somerset Maugham's *The Circle* for Broadway, and he wanted me to come in the following Monday to audition for the role of the ingénue. My heart skipped a beat, and I of course said yes.

The following Monday I auditioned and landed the role. This was my first big break. The production also starred Glynis Johns and Stewart Granger, true old-time movie stars who, along with Sir Rex, were in the later stages of their careers. Between them they had so much experience and wisdom. We toured the country for three months and then ended up on Broadway for a six-month run.

I will never forget that first performance on the Broadway stage in New York. Taking my bow at curtain call, I was overcome with emotion. I was grateful to God for guiding me; to my mother, who instilled in me the love of theater; to my father, who gave me the belief that I had wings and could fly; and to the three angels who had helped put me through drama school.

Because of all of them and their love and support and belief in me, I saw my dreams come true that night.

And that was just the beginning. Appearing on Broadway in *The Circle* led to the title role in *A Woman Named Jackie*, which gave me the courage to move to Los Angeles. Which, of course, would eventually lead to me being cast on *Touched by an Angel.*

Nothing gets going from a stationary position. Energy begets energy; one thing leads to another. Each step of my journey opened the door for the next step, which led to Rex Harrison seeing me, which led me to my dream. Sometimes we say no to opportunities because they may not be exactly what we are looking for. But the truth is you never know where things might lead. You've got to stay open and have faith.

Life as an actor means living with a degree of uncertainty. It's a life that can create self-doubt and upset the natural urge we all have to feel safe. But we have to be bold and brave, because if we are not, we may miss the opportunity to do really great things.

> *It's life, Sidda. You don't figure it out. You just climb up on the beast and ride.*
>
> REBECCA WELLS

I used to think I needed to have all my ducks lined up in a row before I could step out, that only when I felt certain of success should I move forward. But the truth is there is no certainty in this life. Pastor Rick Warren once said, "Living by faith isn't living with certainty. It's trusting God in spite of unanswered questions and unresolved doubts." If I had not put my trust in God, I never would have moved to New York or to Los Angeles.

Living a life of faith means learning to get our feet wet. When Jesus walked on water, only one disciple asked to join him: Peter. Peter slowly stepped out of the boat and began to do the impossible. When he looked down and began to doubt, Jesus stretched out his hand and encouraged him to trust, to look only at Him. And Peter walked on water.

I once heard someone say that the only difference between excitement and fear is your attitude.

Peter was afraid. But at least he got out of the boat.

Our God is not one who is content to keep us in our comfort zone. Jesus challenged his disciples to do more than they thought possible. The disciples weren't cut from theological cloth or raised on supernatural milk. But they were an ounce more devoted than they were afraid, and, as a result, did some extraordinary things.

MAX LUCADO

The Truelove

There is a faith in loving fiercely
the one who is rightfully yours,
especially if you have
waited years and especially
if part of you never believed
you could deserve this
loved and beckoning hand
held out to you this way.

I am thinking of faith now
and the testaments of loneliness
and what we feel we are
worthy of in this world.

Years ago in the Hebrides
I remember an old man
who walked every morning
on the grey stones
to the shore of baying seals,

who would press his hat
to his chest in the blustering
salt wind and say his prayer
to the turbulent Jesus
hidden in the water,

and I think of the story
of the storm and everyone
waking and seeing
the distant
yet familiar figure,
far across the water
calling to them,

and how we are all
waiting for that
abrupt waking, and that calling,
and that moment
when we have to say *yes*,
except it will
not come so grandly,
so Biblically,
but more subtly
and intimately, in the face
of the one you know
you have to love.

So that when
we finally step out of the boat
toward them, we find
everything holds
us, and everything confirms
our courage, and if you wanted
to drown you could,
but you don't,

because finally,
after all this struggle
and all these years,
you don't want to anymore,
you've simply had enough
of drowning,
and you want to live and you
want to love and you will
walk across any territory
and any darkness,
however fluid and however
dangerous, to take the
one hand you know
belongs in yours.

David Whyte

THE BIBLE PROJECT

Dream big and dare to fail.

NORMAN VAUGHAN

When *Touched by an Angel* wrapped after nine glorious seasons, my daughter, Reilly, who was six and a half at the time, and I moved back to Los Angeles. I wasn't sure what was to come next, but I was ready for a bit of downtime. I had worked consistently for almost a decade with hardly any time off, and I was tired. I needed some quiet space so I could gather myself, trusting that I would be guided to the next thing.

I enrolled Reilly in school; we found a lovely, welcoming church; and life began to find a new rhythm. Then, not long after returning to L.A., when I least expected it, I met Mark. We fell in love and knew we wanted to spend the rest of our lives together, so we married and merged our young families together. Mark and I hadn't worked together before, but of course we were in similar fields. He was producing television shows, and at that time had already achieved incredible success with the reality show *Survivor*. But we both longed for a chance to work on something together and hoped to incorporate our faith into that work. I had had the privilege of bringing my faith to my work for all those years on *Touched by an Angel*, and I wanted my work life and faith life to be aligned again.

As a family, we loved watching movies together. Given our professions, we watched a lot of new movies, but every now and then we would pull out an old classic. One year, around Easter, we put on *The Ten Commandments* and gathered as a family in front of the television set. But the film did not hold our young children's interest like we thought it would. Having been made over sixty years earlier, the film was just too old-fashioned for them; and while it is, of course, one of the classics, the truth is that our kids found it outdated and a bit slow.

One morning a few weeks after this, as we were sitting on our porch having a cup of tea, I mentioned to Mark: "You know, no one has ever done the Bible as a television show. We should do that."

Mark looked at me and laughed. "What, the whole thing?"

I laughed, too. "Well, there is certainly a beginning and an end. We'd just have to figure out what stories to include in the middle."

That conversation was the first step in one of the largest undertakings in our professional careers.

It was truly a Herculean task, to take a thousand-page document, beloved and revered by so many people, and bring it to the small screen in a way that honored our faith and glorified God. But what an exciting opportunity to bring these stories to life for a whole new generation. I felt ready to step outside my role as an actor and step into the role of producer.

Mark and I spent hours together, imagining what it could be. If we were going to pitch this idea, we had to know exactly what it was going to entail. The New Testament felt easier to figure out, as it has a clear narrative beginning with Jesus' birth and ending with his death and resurrection. But the Old Testament is more challenging. It spans so many years and has countless characters. There were obviously some stories we knew we had to incorporate, and then we had a wish list of others we thought might work well on the screen.

We soon reached out to a friend of ours, the president of Pepperdine University, and asked him to gather some of the theologians on his staff to be a sounding board about the project. We had an incredible meeting with these bright and faithful minds. They were encouraging but agreed it would be challenging. They promised to begin praying for us immediately.

You miss 100 percent of the shots you don't take.

WAYNE GRETZKY

When we would mention this project to other friends, we wouldn't always get such encouragement. In fact, many of our friends tried to dissuade us from pursuing it. They thought we were nuts. *It's too risky, too big, what if you get it wrong, it could be dangerous or you might look foolish. You*

can't win, you will fail. No one cares about the Bible anymore.
No one will buy it in Hollywood, and it could be a big, noisy,
humiliating flop!

We heard their concerns and didn't necessarily disagree
with them. We called in prayer, and we moved forward
in faith. We chose to listen
to the positive whisper of
encouragement in our hearts
rather than the loud negative
noises of the outside world.

There is only one way to
avoid criticism: do nothing,
say nothing, and be
nothing.

ARISTOTLE

Eventually we found the
perfect partners at the His-
tory channel and Hearst. The team at History immediately
understood our hope for the scope and scale of the series,
and they stepped up and partnered with us. We compiled a
very large team of Bible consultants and theologians to make
sure we brought the story to life accurately. Our intention
was to bring the global audience closer to God through these
amazing stories.

As the writers were shaping the scripts, we began casting
in London and Los Angeles and scouting locations; and before we knew it, we were set to begin filming in Morocco.

Yet one cast member eluded us.

We were just weeks from beginning principal photogra-
phy, and we had not yet cast our most important role: Jesus.
To say this made us nervous would be an understatement. He
was, after all, our leading man.

Obviously it takes a special actor to portray Jesus, who is so much more than a character or historical figure. This person must have the special presence to portray someone both human and divine. In addition, he must be ready and willing to take on the role, which would be both daunting and difficult.

I was beginning to get worried, and I reached out to all my friends and church prayer circles with an email whose subject line made us all smile: "Looking for Jesus." I prayed fervently, asking God to send me the perfect actor to play the Lord, and then to let me know him when he showed up. Then, through a remarkable series of "coincidences," I was sent a videotape of an actor reading on camera. It got my attention right away, and the small voice within me told me to follow up. I found out the tape was of the Portuguese actor Diogo Morgado.

I called his agent and asked whether he could come in for a meeting. His agent thought I was calling from London and said, "I'm so sorry, but Diogo is out of the country right now."

"Where is he?" I asked.

"He's in L.A.," the agent replied.

I laughed out loud. "That's where I am," I said with glee. "Can he come by my home office tomorrow?" I asked.

"I'll find out," the agent said.

Sure enough, he was able to come.

I was waiting in the hallway with Mark when we received the call that Diogo had arrived. We have glass on our front door, so we were able to peek out as we watched Diogo open the garden gate and walk up the path to our house.

As he approached, a huge monarch butterfly the size of a small bird swooped down in front of his face, almost knocking him off his feet.

I was sure it was a sign.

I started to laugh and turned to Mark, who knew exactly what I was thinking. "There he is, Mark," I said with a smile. "There is our Jesus."

And Diogo walked through the door and into our lives.

If there had been any doubt in my mind before, it was all gone now—I believed that butterfly was a sign from God.

When *The Bible* finally began airing on the History channel in the spring of 2013, it exceeded everyone's expectations. The ratings were incredible, with over 100 million people eventually viewing it. Even more special was the personal feedback we began to receive from people around the country. They shared what it was like to watch these impactful stories together as a family and how it created an opportunity to discuss matters of faith with their kids. People were talking about Jesus around the water cooler. They were talking about *The Bible* on talk shows and morning shows; it was such a blessing to see how the series was being used to touch people's hearts and remind them of God's love.

Shortly thereafter, Mark and I were honored with the chance to speak at the National Prayer Breakfast in Washington, D.C., to an audience of leaders from all around the world, including the then president of the United States, Barack Obama. We talked about undertaking this project and the significance of bringing the Bible to national television, and shared about our own personal faith and what it felt like to be called "the noisiest Christians in Hollywood." We knew that with that title came great risk and great responsibility.

I think back to those many conversations with people who tried to convince us we would regret pursuing this project. They had only seen the reasons to be afraid.

I am sure that it helped that there were two of us. I'm so thankful I had Mark by my side. I know that pursuing this task together strengthened us in our resolve to move forward, and, I think, strengthened our marriage and friendship as well. I can't help but feel that God brought us together "for such a time as this."

Two was better than one, and together with God's help, we knew we could do it.

I hereby command you: Be strong and courageous; do not be frightened or dismayed, for the Lord your God is with you wherever you go.

JOSHUA 1:9 (NRSV)

That we are here is a huge affirmation; somehow life needed us and wanted us to be. To sense and trust this primeval acceptance can open a vast spring of trust within the heart. It can free us into a natural courage that casts out fear and opens up our lives to become voyages of discovery, creativity, and compassion. No threshold need be a threat, but rather an invitation and a promise. Whatever comes, the great sacrament of life will remain faithful to us, blessing us always with visible signs of invisible grace. We merely need to trust.

John O'Donohue

CARRIED IN HIS ARMS

God invites us to experience our not
being in control as an invitation to faith.

HENRI NOUWEN

I've always loved the poem "Footprints." My father first shared it with me shortly after my mother's death. It reminded me of the song my mother used to sing to me as I was falling asleep, "You'll Never Walk Alone." Ever since I was a little girl, I've kept a copy of the "Footprints" poem in credit-card size in my wallet, just in case I encounter someone who needs encouragement. Then I share it with them.

As I prepared to go to Morocco for the filming of *The Bible*, I knew I wasn't going to take my normal wallet. I was going to take only the essentials into the desert with me, and I certainly wouldn't need all my membership cards, credit cards, and Starbucks cards! For some reason, I plucked the "Footprints" card out of my wallet and stuffed it into the little bag that would go with me on the film set. Perhaps someone during the course of shooting might need it.

Morocco is beautiful, but the climate can be very challenging, with searing-hot sun during the day and sometimes freezing-cold temperatures in the evenings. Mark had been with me for the first couple of weeks, but he was in the middle of producing the NBC hit music show *The Voice* and needed to fly back to L.A. for the taping. We had a very skilled team in place, so while I would miss him, I knew I could handle things on the set while he was gone.

One day we were preparing to film the scene where Abraham walks up the mountain to sacrifice his son, Isaac. It is one of the most powerful and dramatic scenes in the Bible. Abraham is so faithful that he is willing to sacrifice his only son, the son that he and Sarah had prayed for, longed for, and that God had finally given to them in their old age. In the scene, we see Abraham trusting God; and even though his heart is breaking, he does not question God and is prepared to do as God asks. Mercifully, an angel of God intervenes and says, "Do not lay your hand on the boy or do anything to him; for now I know that you fear God, since you have not withheld your son, your only son, from me" (Genesis 22:12, NRSV). And before Abraham's eyes, there appears a lamb, the lamb he is now to sacrifice instead of his beloved son.

Obviously, we needed a lamb to film this scene, and in

What do you do when alone with God?
Many of us think, talk or ask.
But when alone with God it's also important to listen!
Solitude is the place where you can
hear the voice that calls you the beloved,
that leads you onto the next page of the adventure,
that says, as God said to Jesus early in the Gospels,
"This is my son, the Beloved,
with whom I am well pleased" (Matt. 3:17).
HENRI NOUWEN

the production meetings to prepare for this episode, I had requested two white lambs (I've learned through filming that you always need a backup animal in case the first one doesn't cooperate). We had reached out to some of the local people helping us with the shoot and requested that two white lambs be on the set first thing in the morning. It was all arranged.

When I arrived at our location that morning, I saw two lambs and a handler. And yet, these were not white lambs. One was a black lamb, and one was, let's just say, muddy-colored at best.

Through the translator, I did my best to communicate with their handler and asked him why he didn't bring a white lamb. But no matter how much I protested, it didn't change the fact that we did not have a white lamb; and because we were filming in such a remote location, it would likely take several hours for this mistake to be remedied.

We did not have several hours. We needed to start filming.

What difference does it make what color the lamb is? I heard someone ask. But I knew that I wanted the lamb to signify Jesus, who came to be sacrificed for us. Jesus as the Lamb of God. Hans Zimmer had written a beautiful piece of music for the scene with Abraham. The music soared as Abraham and Isaac carried the wood up the hill for the sacrifice. We would play this same music in a later scene as Jesus carried the wood of the cross on which He would be sacrificed. The white lamb was significant and important.

I tried to hide it, but inside I was incredibly frustrated, thinking about how this would throw off our filming schedule for the entire day.

I walked off the set, feeling irritated and alone. I knew if I didn't take a moment to breathe and pray, I was going to cry.

I reached into my purse to grab a tissue, and the "Footprints" poem fell out.

I picked it up and began to read it for the thousandth time. When I got to the end, I smiled and thanked God for this reminder. I hadn't realized when I packed it that I was the one who would need it. That it was there for me. That in the middle of this arid desert, where we were trying to create this series to honor God and His story, I was the one who would need this reminder.

I'm here with you. I'm carrying you. You are never alone.

With my faith restored, I rejoined the team. We decided that we would film with the muddy-colored lamb and change his color in postproduction. It would require coming back to this very location with a white lamb so we could shoot a plate that we would drop into the scene with special effects at a later stage. But at least we had a plan for the day. God helped to keep me calm so that I could make a plan and move forward.

I believe that with faith, we can each do the impossible— that life is waiting for us to step up, believe, and do great things. There are always going to be times of anxiety and fear. But when we learn that even in those times, God is with us, it makes it all more tolerable. I've learned that God sometimes calms the storm, but at other times He lets the storm rage and calms the child. So when you feel like you are drowning in the sea of life, just remember that your lifeguard walks on water.

When I stand before God at the end of my life, I would hope that I would not have a single bit of talent left, and could say, "I used everything you gave me."

ERMA BOMBECK

May I dare to
dream big,
to see possibilities
instead of limits,
to believe that you, God,
can do impossible things
with your willing children.
Sometimes, God, I get afraid,
and I'd rather stay safe
than do what my
heart is calling me to do.
Please, Lord, help me
to reach out,
to get out of the boat,
and when I fear that
I'm sinking,
drowning, 
look up, see you,
and keep walking in faith.

Spread love everywhere you go. Let no one ever come to you without leaving happier.

MOTHER TERESA

Dear friends, let us love one another, for love comes from God. Everyone who loves has been born of God and knows God.

1 JOHN 4:7 (NIV)

four

LOVE

What we have once enjoyed, we can never lose.
All that we love deeply becomes part of us.

HELEN KELLER

I WAITED for a long time to have my daughter. I had always assumed I would have children one day but never felt the time was right. There was always one more mountain to climb, one more task to accomplish, and of course there was the question of finding the right mate.

A couple of years after I first moved to Los Angeles, I began dating a wonderful man. David was a film director, and we went on a blind date, set up by a friend of mine. We quickly fell in love. Within a few months, I booked the role of Monica and realized that I would be moving to Utah to film the show; so after we got married, he split his time between Utah and L.A. His work was in L.A., as well as his lovely seventeen-year-old daughter, Vanessa. I was already thirty-five by then, and so I knew that if we were to have children of our own, there was no time to delay.

When I found out that I was pregnant, we were both thrilled, and I couldn't wait to tell my other family, the cast and crew of *Touched by an Angel*.

The day came when I felt ready to share my news. We were filming in a jazz club, of all places, and the legendary musician B. B. King was on set. We had been filming onstage and had a lull in the action, so I told B. B. that I had some special news to share with the group. He said, "Can I play a little intro to get their attention?" and I smiled and said yes. He began to play his guitar, and everyone on set turned to see what was going on. When B. B. finished his musical introduction, I turned back to the cast and crew and said, "Well, thanks, B. B., for that lovely introduction to some wonderful news. I'm so thrilled to share with you all—you who have become my trusted friends and who are truly like family to me— that we are adding one more little angel to the family. I'm pregnant!"

Everyone cheered as B. B. began to play again. I turned around, and he came over and began to play to my tummy. My eyes filled with tears with the special introduction my precious baby was getting to the world.

We had quite an interesting time on the series keeping my pregnancy hidden from viewers. Given our filming schedule, we were expected to shoot until early May, and I was due in June. So there were countless scenes where I was carrying coats or large sun hats or shopping bags, or standing behind open car doors or a couch. With other kinds of shows, a pregnancy might have been written into the script, but that wasn't an option since I was playing an angel!

I chose not to find out whether we were having a boy or a girl, wanting that miraculous surprise at the moment my child was born. But the truth is, when I heard the words "It's a girl!" I realized just how much I had been hoping for a daughter. And here she was now, in my arms. My own precious, beautiful child.

I named her Reilly, to honor the memory of my mother, Maureen O'Reilly.

As I stared down at my sweet baby girl, I felt something happen within me. Tears streamed down my face, both for the miracle that I held in my arms and for the fact that something I so desperately missed was now restored. I cried in that moment for the mother I had lost and the mother I had now become. I had been filled with longing my whole life for this mother-daughter relationship. Now, with Reilly's birth, I was given a second chance at that relationship, a relationship I had been missing for more than half of my life. When my mother died, I missed her so much that there was truly a hole in me; the woman I became just grew up around that "hole." But it was as if Reilly's birth put a "W" in front of that word and made me "whole" again. As I held my beautiful baby girl in my arms, I cried tears of joy and healing. There is no question that love is a healer. It began in that hospital room;

and in the years since, the love has filled me and touched all the old hurts within me. The love Reilly brought to my life has ultimately healed me. She is my special angel. My sweet, beautiful girl. My gift from God.

Motherhood opened up a deep well of love in me, love I didn't know I had access to. Becoming a mother also helped my faith grow and deepen because it has given me insight into how much God loves us. His unconditional love, His perfect loving. I finally understood just how much God loves each and every one of us. We are, after all, His special children. The depth of my love for Reilly amazes me. And, of course, I then marvel at God's love for us.

Even though Reilly was born by caesarian section, I had to go back to work just a few short weeks after her birth. But I was blessed to have had the help and support of so many. I'm thankful for Debbie, our amazing nanny, and everyone on set who made me feel so loved. I could not have done it without Linda, my assistant, and the wonderful cast and crew who cared for us. And I was gifted with a schedule that offered some downtime, when I could rock and feed and love on my little baby girl in between my time filming.

Della was a doting grandmother, and our other regular cast member, John Dye, was the perfect, loving Uncle Johnnie. He always called Reilly his little lamb. In the embrace of this extended and loving family, Reilly grew and blossomed; but sadly, the same cannot be said for my marriage to her dad. My dreams of happily ever after were crushed around the time Reilly turned one. We decided to separate, and by the time she turned two, we had divorced.

So for many years, it was just the two of us. Reilly's dad came to visit her every few weeks, and he was always a good dad and a loving part of her life, but for the day-to-day of it, I was a single mom. Of course we always had Della by our side. I sometimes had family visits from Ireland, when my two half sisters, Ann and Jacinta, would come on their vacations. Reilly always loved the visits from her Irish aunties. But for the most part it was me, my girl, and our two doggies in our big house in Utah. We were best buddies

You don't know what unconditional love is. You may say you do, but if you don't have a child, you don't know what that is. But when you experience it, it is the most fulfilling experience ever.

REGINA KING

and so incredibly close. We spent all our time together. Once while shopping in a local mall, someone asked me for an autograph. Reilly, who was only four at the time, tugged at my hand and said, "This is *my* mommy, not TV mommy."

Reilly and I had such fun together. We had tea parties for her dolls and stuffed animals, we painted pictures, we played hopscotch, and we pretended to be characters in the movies we watched together while curled up on the couch. We swam in the summer, and we built snowmen in the winter. I adored her and passed all my loving and nurturing into my sweet little girl. I knew Reilly was sometimes confused about the fact

My Little Angel

Oh, my little angel,
you are the flesh and blood
of my flesh and my blood.
It was God who breathed life into you,
and, for me, that was His greatest gift of all.

And now as I watch you sleeping,
I'm still lost in wonder
at the miracle of your birth,
and lost for words to describe
the blessings you have brought me.

Where once my life seemed sometimes empty and futile,
now you fill me up and give me reason to live.

In a world full of suspicion, dishonesty, and distrust,
you, my little angel, are an open book.

When I am weak, you give me strength;
when I am drifting, you are my anchor.

Yesterday I found you weeping over a broken doll,
and I wanted to cry as I held you in my arms.

And when the day comes that I find you
weeping over a broken heart,
I know I'll want to die,
but I'll still be here to comfort you.

Oh, my little angel,
whate'er befalls you in the years ahead,
may the Lord above, who gave you to me,
hold you in the hollow of His hand.

Phil Coulter

that our family didn't look like a traditional family. I knew she longed to have a mom and dad and siblings who all lived together as other children do. Her dad and sister, Vanessa, lived in another state, and though she saw them regularly, it wasn't the same. One day a little girl at school said that we weren't a real family because it was just the two of us. That upset Reilly, and she came home to me in tears.

I tried to explain that no matter what, it's *love* that defines a family. I tried to share how much I felt like Della Reese was my mama, no matter that we came from two different places. I went on to tell Reilly about the fact that my family didn't look "normal" growing up, as I lost my mother when I was ten; so I was a little girl without a mother, and with just my dad to raise us. Other family members helped out when they could, but my father really was a single parent again. He learned to braid my long hair and took me shopping for dresses, and he never wanted me to feel the void that was obviously there from missing Mom. Bless him, he strove so hard to make things okay.

This story seemed to comfort Reilly. She held me tight and said, "It's you and me, Mama. We are a family." I kissed her little head and reassured her, "Yes, baby, I will love you forever, and I will always be your mommy."

I tried to show Reilly that she was part of a big family, too, by taking her to Ireland once a year so we could see my siblings and she could play with her many Irish cousins. I wanted her to know what it means to be Irish, to know the richness of our culture and beauty of our country, since it is such an integral part of who I consider myself to be.

It was a few more years before Reilly and I found the family we'd always dreamed of. And when we did, it was so fun and joyful to be welcomed into the family of Burnetts and feel like we all belonged together. We blended two families into one, often joking that we were like the Brady Bunch; we all felt so fortunate to have found one another. We weren't a traditional family, so we felt that much more special. We had created something of our own, had taken what could have been just wounds and made something beautiful from them. Love is a healer, a mender. Love has the power to make things whole.

The Beatles were right. All you need is love. Love makes a family, not DNA or background. Love. Just love. Simply love.

All those years ago, as I was in the midst of my divorce, heartbroken and hurting, I didn't know what was to come. I didn't know then that many years later, I would sit at my Thanksgiving table, under the tree in my garden, with my family, my husband and my daughter and my two fine stepsons. And that one year we would also include my ex-husband and his nephew, and my husband's ex-wife and her father, and we would all break bread together, and hold hands and pray, and be thankful to God together for the blessings we have, and for the gift of family, no matter what it looks like.

*We must let go of the life we have planned,
so as to accept the one that is waiting for us.*

JOSEPH CAMPBELL

For a Mother-to-Be

Nothing could have prepared
Your heart to open like this.

From beyond the skies and the stars
This echo arrived inside you
And started to pulse with life,
Each beat a tiny act of growth,
Traversing all our ancient shapes
On its way home to itself.

Once it began, you were no longer your own.
A new, more courageous you, offering itself
In a new way to a presence you can sense
But you have not seen or known.

It has made you feel alone
In a way you never knew before;
Everyone else sees only from the outside
What you feel and feed
With every fiber of your being.

Never have you traveled farther inward
Where words and thoughts become half-light
Unable to reach the fund of brightness
Strengthening inside the night of your womb.

Like some primeval moon,
Your soul brightens
The tides of essence
That flow to your child.

You know your life has changed forever,
For in all the days and years to come,
Distance will never be able to cut you off
From the one you now carry
For nine months under your heart.

May you be blessed with quiet confidence
That destiny will guide you and mind you.

May the emerging spirit of your child
Imbibe encouragement and joy
From the continuous music of your heart,
So that it can grow with ease,
Expectant of wonder and welcome
When its form is fully filled

And it makes its journey out
To see you and settle at last
Relieved, and glad in your arms.

John O'Donohue

LOVE STORY

I love you without knowing how, or when, or from where.
I love you simply, without problems or pride:
I love you in this way because I do not know
any other way of loving but this, in which there is no I or you,
so intimate that your hand upon my chest is my hand,
so intimate that when I fall asleep your eyes close.

PABLO NERUDA

The most magical things can have the humblest of beginnings.

The magic of my love story with Mark began with my feet in a bucket of water. Not the most glamorous of images, I know, but a girl needs a pedicure every now and then!

I had recently moved back to Los Angeles after wrapping nine seasons of *Touched by an Angel.* I was being very prayerful and thoughtful about the next steps in my career. I didn't want to plunge ahead without God's gentle guidance. It was a time of great soul-searching and of discovering a deeper sense of self, now free of the attention that had rained down on me during the success of *Touched by an Angel.* For nine years, I had been in the limelight, on countless magazine covers, doing daytime and nighttime talk shows, walking the red carpet, and receiving accolades and awards. I had tried very hard to stay grounded and in gratitude during that time; but the truth is, when it all goes away, it can feel very quiet. The silence can be deafening. In my industry, you can be recognized as one of *People* magazine's "Most Beautiful People in the World" one year, and the next year get no public attention at all. If you don't have a strong sense of self or a spiritual life, you can feel adrift and lost. If you don't have a sense of humor, the lack of attention can be painful. And let's face it, if you allow yourself to be defined by what you do, then it raises the question, Who are you when you aren't doing that?

Most of us know in our heads that our sense of self should not be dependent on what we do or how we look. But in real life, that's hard to pull off. I look at my daughter and her friends, and it pains me to see the pressure these girls feel to be thin or beautiful. Our culture puts such an unhealthy emphasis on looking a certain way in order to be loved or valued.

I know firsthand how illusory beauty is. Over the years I appeared on magazine covers, but it wasn't me just showing up with that kind of beauty. There was always a hair and makeup team and a stylist selecting beautiful clothes.

But young women don't realize how fake this beauty is. They see it and think they should look that way.

I wanted to instill in Reilly an appreciation for real beauty.

Real beauty is of the heart; it's the glow that lights your face when you are doing something kind, it's the tears you cry in appreciation of someone else's pain. Real beauty is kindness, gratitude, love.

If you get too attached to being beautiful on the outside, what happens when that "beauty" starts to fade? As we naturally age, fear can start to emerge. It can be a painful struggle, and I am not immune to this fear. Fear of letting go of that illusion of beauty. Fear of no longer being valued and accepted.

But the real freedom is to be found in letting go of fear. Letting go of the need to look a certain way, to be accepted by the masses. Who you are is perfect. God made you that way. He loves who you are becoming on the inside. This body will fade away. That's what it was made to do.

Your heart and spirit will be with you forever.

If we can remember this, fear dissolves.

Consider Mother Teresa, a woman who aged gracefully and didn't let it slow her down. Her beauty was apparent until the day she died. It glowed in the warmth of her smile as she helped God's people. She was radiant. She emitted a light that you cannot buy in a bottle.

She displayed the true beauty of grace, compassion, and love.

I knew that this time in Malibu—in between my role as Monica and whatever God had planned for me next— was an important season of growth . . . a time of letting go of the experience of *Touched by an Angel* and the deep connection I had to playing and being Monica, and a time of expanding and deepening my understanding of self and trusting in God for whatever was next. In fact, I discovered a beautiful sense of freedom after we moved back to Malibu and I enrolled Reilly in the local grade school. I loved being Mom at the park and queen of the carpool and living a normal life. I didn't know what was next, but I knew God would guide me.

One afternoon, Della came over for lunch. And in her sweet, direct way, she said, "Are you lonely, baby? Isn't it time you trusted your heart to love again?"

Well, I felt very happy with my life the way it was. "Oh, I don't know about that. It's hard to meet quality guys," I said, shaking my head.

"Well, honey, it's simple. You've got to hand it over. You have to ask God to choose a partner for you."

I laughed. It was simple, but I hadn't ever thought of that. I'd never really thought to ask God to choose for me.

Della said, "Well, think about what you want, and you bring that to God. Don't pray it over and over. Pray it once, and then just trust."

As usual, Della, the great loving and wise woman, was guiding me in a way that I am so thankful for.

And so I took some time to think about what I truly wanted in a man. I would be mindful of those qualities and pay attention. I wanted a man who would be strong and caring, a man to love me and my daughter, and a man who loved God. I wanted a man who was kind and loving and funny. I wanted a good man, an honest man, a man with integrity. I wanted him to be smart and to have his own success so there wouldn't be anything competitive between us. I wanted a man who would make me feel safe. I wanted him to love kids, and I wanted him to share my love of the ocean, of Ireland . . . to be honest, it was a long list!

And then I took a moment and picked up my list and handed it over to God. "God, this is what I think I need, but I didn't choose well in the past, so all I ask is that you let me know when he gets here."

So on an ordinary afternoon, a few months later, I was getting a pedicure in a salon. And as I sat there with my feet in a bucket of water, wearing a tracksuit with an elastic waistband, for goodness' sake, I noticed a man getting his hair cut across the room from me. His back was to me, but I noticed him because he was laughing a lot and generally being pretty noisy. My eyes caught his in the mirror, and my heart started to race. I mean, it was racing. I couldn't ignore it. And I thought, *Really? Is this happening?*

I quickly looked away, embarrassed that he had caught me watching. But I looked up again, and our eyes met again. I felt my cheeks heat. He was so handsome and joyful. Again I thought, *Really, is that him?* and I stared back down at my book. I had never reacted this way to seeing someone before. It was a physical reaction, like my body was trying to let me know . . . *something is happening here. Pay attention.*

I couldn't help myself. My eyes were drawn back to the mirror one more time. And yet again, he was looking at me!

I vowed not to make that mistake again.

A few minutes later, his haircut was finished, he spent a few moments checking out with the receptionist, and he was gone.

When my nails were dry, I carefully put on my flip-flops and walked up to the same checkout desk.

My curiosity got the best of me.

"Excuse me," I said to the receptionist, casually. "But do you happen to know the name of the man who just walked out of here?"

She looked at me with a smile. "Oh, isn't that funny," she said, "he just asked me who *you* were."

We laughed together, and she told me his name was Mark Burnett. He was local, but originally from the UK; he was divorced with two little kids and was a producer of reality TV.

I thanked her for letting me know and wondered when he might show back up in my life. He certainly had piqued my interest.

A few days later, I got a call from that receptionist. Mark had called the salon and asked if they might give him my number. She, of course, wanted to check with me first, before giving out personal information.

I said, "Yes, please give him my number!"

Shortly after that, she called back again.

"Yes?" I said, confused.

"I'm sorry to bother you again, but he wanted me to ask whether you would say yes if he called and asked you out?" the receptionist said with a laugh, probably feeling a bit like a schoolyard go-between, stuck back in the seventh grade.

I had to admit, I found it kind of adorable that he had her call and ask me that. I told her she could give him my number; of course I was going to say yes!

Well, a few moments later, he called, we went out, and I soon realized that this was it. My love had arrived.

Our first date was a Stevie Wonder concert at the House of Blues. Mark and I hit it off immediately. We both came from the same corner of the world, were born the same year, were both divorced with young children of a similar age (he had two boys, I had my little girl). We were both self-made, working in the same field. We lived on the same beach, drove the same car, laughed at the same jokes. It was better than anything I had ever experienced. It was the kind of love I knew could last my entire life.

We were married in a small ceremony presided over by Della, with just our new little family in attendance, and Mark's dad, Archie, and stepmom, Jean. Our oldest boy, James, served as best man; our little boy, Cameron, as ring bearer; and my beautiful Reilly was my bridesmaid. It was not just the marriage of two people but the coming together of a family of five. It felt like it was meant to be. Each child got to keep his or her position in the family. James was still the oldest, Cameron still the youngest, Reilly still the only girl.

We said our vows under a beautiful arbor in our backyard, where I had entwined three silk butterflies to represent my parents and Mark's mom, our angels in attendance. But they also made their presence known in other ways. That morning, as Mark and I gazed out at the ocean, saying prayers of gratitude for the special day that was under way, three butterflies fluttered right in front of us, a sign of God's presence and our loved ones' spirits. When Della arrived, she carried with her an ornate purse with butterflies embroidered on it. And finally, later in the day, despite the fact that we hadn't shared the news of our wedding with any of our friends, planning instead to send a marriage announcement after the fact, a gift arrived via FedEx, and within was a picture frame with three butterflies in the corner.

God made it clear that He was with us and blessing us with this day.

We had such a lovely time creating a new family from our five disparate parts. I love kids and had always wanted more children, and here I had these two beautiful young boys in my life! James and Cameron are a blessing to me. We certainly had to make some adjustments—Reilly had to learn to play with the boys and be a part of a larger family, since it had been just the two of us for so long. And the boys had to learn what it was like to have a sister in their lives. I'll never forget one morning, a few months after we were married, when everyone was rushing around, getting ready for school. Reilly and I were walking down the stairs as Mark was trying to get James and Cameron to find their backpacks, and in Mark's noisy fashion, he used a louder tone than Reilly was accustomed to with me. She looked at me and said, "Mom, I can't believe you fell in love with a military man!"

Oh, how I laughed. Mark had served time in the British military, which I know impacted the man he is today and how he handles himself, but to hear my little girl put it that way just cracked me up. We still laugh about it today.

Now, of course, all three of our lovely children are grown, and Mark and I are practically empty nesters. They are each following their own dreams. Reilly is back east at college studying theater, James recently graduated and is pursuing his love of the music business, and Cameron is in film school. It is so special to see them all making their way in the world, pursuing their dreams; but we're so happy when they take the time to come back home so we can be together as a family—as we know not to take family for granted.

As I look back, I know I got the family I'd always dreamed of; but I also got so much more. For Mark and I became not just husband and wife together, not just parents together, not just best friends, although all of those have made me happier than I could ever have dreamed. Mark and I also became business partners. We had the privilege of making *The Bible* together—it was a large, challenging undertaking but also a project that came to affect so many people. We went on to create our production company, LightWorkers Media, and produced many TV series and films together. We truly believe God brought us together to create such projects and bring them into the world, to shine a light for such a time as this. God's plans are so much bigger than we could have imagined. Isn't that always the case? Our vision can be small, while He is working things together for a greater good, the ultimate good. Our partnership has

> *Love does not consist in gazing at each other, but in looking outward together in the same direction.*
> ANTOINE DE SAINT-EXUPÉRY

helped to deepen our marriage and our friendship. We are so grateful that, with God's help, we found each other.

The love I share with Mark is the love I've always dreamed of receiving. He loves me the way I always wanted to be loved. One story provides a great example of this. About ten years ago, all five of us were in Australia together as a family. The boys were thirteen and nine, and Reilly was about ten. And as we wandered the streets of Sydney, we saw a little painting in the window of an art gallery. I don't remember who saw it first, but we were all soon gathered around this window, marveling at this particular piece of art. It was a small painting of a dog that looked just like our great big Irish wolfhound, Finn. And surrounding the dog were three but-terflies.

Of course my entire family knows how much I love butterflies and how symbolic they have been in my life. We all marveled at the dog's resemblance to Finn, and how there were three butterflies, one for each of the children.

After a bit of conversation and much laughter, we kept walking, exploring the town.

That afternoon, as we went back to the hotel for a rest, I sneaked back to the little gallery. It was June, and Mark's birthday was in July. I wanted to get the painting for him as a birthday surprise.

If God only used perfect people, nothing would get done. God will use anybody if you're available.

RICK WARREN

When I got back to the hotel with the painting, the kids were lying around a tad jet-lagged, reading and relaxing, and Mark was in the other room on the phone. So I quietly showed the kids my surprise, and then quickly buried it in the bottom of my suitcase.

The next month, as I handed Mark his present, he opened it with care and then looked up at me with delight when he saw what was inside.

"I can't believe it!" he said, with a laugh.

"I know, I just had to get it for you," I said, remembering our trip and our family's joy in the discovery.

"No, no, you don't understand," Mark said, shaking his head with a smile. "I went back the next day to buy the painting for *you* because you had loved it so much. But it was already gone."

My mouth dropped open in shock. Cameron piped in at this point.

"He took me with him, and I had to pretend I didn't know you had already bought it!" he said.

Mark's eyes met mine. We smiled and laughed, that we had each had this same instinct to do something loving for the other one. It reminded me of that lovely O. Henry story "The Gift of the Magi." She sells her hair to buy him a chain for his watch, but he has sold his watch to buy beautiful combs for her hair. I know without a doubt that love is a verb. Anyone can say the words "I love you," but love is an action. Mark and I had the same loving instinct for each other.

This is how good love can be.

I sometimes marvel at the blessings in my life, but none more than my partnership with Mark. It was always my greatest dream to find someone who loved me the same way I loved him. I have that in Mark.

Thank you, God.

> *The minute I heard my first love story*
> *I started looking for you, not knowing*
> *how blind that was.*
> *Lovers don't finally meet somewhere.*
> *They're in each other all along.*
>
> RUMI

My children, our love should not be only words and talk. Our love must be true love. And we should show that love by what we do.

1 JOHN 3:18 (ICB)

THE MOTHER OF GOD

Love anything and your heart will be wrung
and possibly broken. If you want to make sure
of keeping it intact you must give it to no one.
To love is to be vulnerable.

C. S. LEWIS

As I shared earlier, it was quite a journey to find our Jesus for the *Bible* series. Once Diogo walked up our drive and into our lives, it felt as if it was meant to be. Both Mark and I felt a deep connection to him and trusted him inherently to take on this important role.

This role required a lot from the actor. Once filming had started, I began the practice of praying before each scene. Diogo would often join me in prayer. Sometimes we would read the scene as it appeared in the Bible first, and then he would walk onto the set; and I knew the Holy Spirit was with him.

As the weeks passed, we were still looking for someone to play Mary, Jesus' mother. We had already cast a beautiful young actress to play Mary for the nativity scene. We now needed someone older, who looked like that actress might look in thirty years and who could play Mary as she walks beside her grown child as He fulfills the mission God has given Him.

I sat in our production office, looking online at links of actresses to be considered. And I just couldn't seem to find the right one. Mark walked in and saw what I was doing. And he looked at me with a twinkle in his eye. "I don't know why you are missing the obvious. You need to take on this role yourself. You've been like a mother to Diogo anyway."

I stared at Mark in shock. I had never even considered it. I was a producer for this series, not an actress.

And yet, as his words sank in, I began to realize he was right. I was believable as an older version of our young Mary. And I, of course, felt very connected to Diogo. I had promised him that if he took the role of Jesus, I would walk with him every step of the way.

I prayed about it that night and felt a knowing and peace. Yes, this was the answer. I was so thankful to Mark for opening my eyes to the solution that had been in front of us all along.

Taking on the role of Mary touched my heart profoundly. It also made me consider her experience in a way I never had before. I had grown up in a household of faith, and since I was a child, I had reflected on Jesus' sacrifice on the cross and was always filled with gratitude to Him. But as I stepped into the role of His Blessed Mother Mary, I suddenly had to watch this scene through the eyes of a mother and feel this scene with a mother's heart. It must have been unbearable for Mary to see her own son being crucified. Yet she showed such faith and courage. I tried to imagine the faith she must have possessed to not completely fall apart at the foot of the cross. There, up there, is her baby boy! There was the son she had raised and nurtured and loved so much.

While Jesus paid the ultimate sacrifice, sweet, tender Mary also made a sacrifice. Oh, how my heart broke while filming that scene. When she runs up to Him as He carries the cross, He falls to the ground, no longer able to carry the heavy wood. And the guards continue to whip Him. Mary reaches out her hand and can only say, "My son!"

In our film, Jesus looks into His mother's eyes and says, "Don't be afraid. Everything is possible with God."

In the darkest of times, Jesus could still see the light. In His most difficult moment, He was still a man of encouragement and faith.

When we see the cross, we are reminded that to be human is to experience pain. But this, too, shall pass.

I will always carry the memory of that moment and the faith Jesus had as He sought to encourage and strengthen His mother, whom He knew was close to despair. We know, too, that the Lord said only seven things from the cross, yet one of those was to the disciple John, telling him to take care of His mother. Even as He was dying, Jesus was loving His mother.

During filming, in the heat of the desert sun, I kept hearing a tune in my head. I started humming it repeatedly and soon realized that this song had been placed on my heart for a reason. The song was the beautiful Mark Lowry and Buddy Greene song "Mary, Did You Know?" I heard it over and over in my mind. And then I paid attention.

I found the song online and began to play it as I watched the scenes between Jesus and His mother in the editing bay. As I worked with Tessa, one of our talented young editors, I felt inspired. The combination of the song and the imagery was powerful. Maybe God could reach people through it.

And Mary said, Behold the handmaid of the Lord; be it unto me according to thy word. And the angel departed from her.

LUKE 1:38 (KJV)

Mark was back in L.A. filming *The Voice* at the time, and one of our favorite singers was a coach on the show. So I sent Mark the edited material, and he shared it with CeeLo Green. CeeLo grew up going to church, and loved the song "Mary, Did You Know?" He decided to record the song for his new Christmas album, and using the edited footage from the *Bible* series, we pulled together a beautiful music video using CeeLo's extraordinary version of this song. It was released on TV and immediately went viral. It gave people the chance to consider the life of Mary in a new way.

Mary said yes to the angel Gabriel, and her "Yes" changed the course of history.

Mary, Did You Know?

Mary, did you know that your Baby Boy would one day walk
on water?
Mary, did you know that your Baby Boy would save our
sons and daughters?
Did you know that your Baby Boy has come to make you
new?
This Child that you delivered will soon deliver you.

Mary, did you know that your Baby Boy will give sight to a
blind man?
Mary, did you know that your Baby Boy will calm the storm
with His hand?
Did you know that your Baby Boy has walked where angels
trod?
When you kiss your little Baby you kiss the face of God?

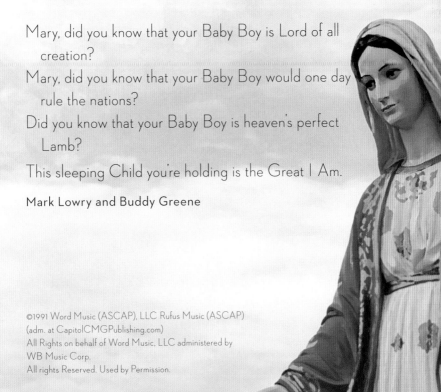

Oh Mary, did you know?

The blind will see, the deaf will hear, the dead will live
  again.
The lame will leap, the dumb will speak the praises of
  The Lamb.

Mary, did you know that your Baby Boy is Lord of all
  creation?
Mary, did you know that your Baby Boy would one day
  rule the nations?
Did you know that your Baby Boy is heaven's perfect
  Lamb?
This sleeping Child you're holding is the Great I Am.

Mark Lowry and Buddy Greene

Mary is a living example of deep, loving surrender, and of the power of sacrifice.

The Blessed Mother inspires all of us to recognize what it means to love God and let go and trust that God always knows best. I know this can be hard sometimes. We strive to control and manage our lives, and it can be a challenge to let go and surrender, to hand it all over to God. But Mary teaches us it is possible. Mary teaches us what love is. Love wants to protect and save, but love also knows that sometimes sacrifice and surrender are what is called for.

When we let go and empty our hands, God is there to fill our open hands.

Think about Mary's darkest days. She didn't know what would happen in three days. That her son would rise from the dead. That His mission was far from over and had, in truth, just begun. Mary trusted God.

This is how we know what love is:
Jesus Christ laid down his life for us.
And we ought to lay down our lives
for our brothers and sisters.

1 JOHN 3:16 (NIV)

AN ANGEL AMONG US

We do not draw people to Christ by loudly
discrediting what they believe, by telling them how wrong
they are and how right we are, but by showing them
a light that is so lovely that they want with all their
hearts to know the source of it.

MADELEINE L'ENGLE

I first met Maya Angelou when she appeared in an episode of *Touched by an Angel* that also featured the lovely and talented Natalie Cole. Della and Maya had been friends for years, and the entire crew was so honored that she agreed to be a part of our show. I had long been an admirer of her and her voice, literally and artistically. She and Della often referred to each other as sisters, and Della had introduced me to her as her "daughter." Maya laughed when she met me. "Well," she said, "since Della and I are sisters, and you are her daughter, I guess that makes me your aunt!"

Meeting her in person did not disappoint. She is one of those people who you just know has much to say. When she spoke, you listened. Even so, she had the gift of giving people her full attention. When she turned her gaze on you, you felt truly seen and heard and recognized. She had an extraordinary gift for raising everyone up and making every single person feel very special. There was a presence about her—of greatness, of humility, of spirit. She embodied her own words: "I have learned that people will forget what you said, people will forget what you did, but people will never forget how you made them feel."

I took Reilly to meet her once, years later when Maya was on tour for her book *Letter to My Daughter*. Maya considered the world her family and each person her child. That is how she looked at you, with eyes full of love and with a heart full of faith and promise. When Reilly met her after her reading, Maya turned her attention to Reilly fully, just as she had to me those many years before back in Utah. It is a moment Reilly has never forgotten.

I also had the chance to visit her a number of times at her home. One time, she was filming a cooking show, and she asked Della and me to appear on it. I flew in the night before and was able to stay at her beautiful home in North Carolina. We sat at her kitchen table, just the two of us, talking and laughing, and then she asked, "Would you care to have me read anything?"

I said, "Oh, yes, anything."

She read "Still I Rise," and then, as a special treat, she read the poem she had written for *Touched by an Angel*. As she began to read, in the quiet half-light of her kitchen, time stood still. It was one of those moments that will forever be imprinted on my heart. Having this amazing woman breathe life into those beautiful words. Just the two of us at her kitchen table drinking tea.

There are people in the world who really get it. Who embody the great possibility that dwells within each one of us. The potential we all have to love, to speak truth, to connect no matter our differences. To understand that we are all one, that we all belong to each other, that we are one big, beautiful family of God.

Maya was one of those people. Maya always said: Be a rainbow in someone else's cloud. Truly, she was an angel.

"Touched by an Angel"
aka
"Love's Exquisite Freedom"

We, unaccustomed to courage
exiles from delight
live coiled in shells of loneliness
until love leaves its high holy temple
and comes into our sight
to liberate us into life.

Love arrives
and in its train come ecstasies
old memories of pleasure
ancient histories of pain.
Yet if we are bold,
love strikes away the chains of fear
from our souls.

We are weaned from our timidity
In the flush of love's light
we dare be brave
And suddenly we see
that love costs all we are
and will ever be.
Yet it is only love
which sets us free.

Maya Angelou

You, God, are love.

We know that love is your essence.

and that you call us

to spread that love.

Help us, Lord.

Help us to become vessels

of your love,

Your peace,

Your kindness,

Your spirit.

Not just to those who

are easy to love,

not just those we

think belong to us,

but all of your children.

May we be part of

a love revolution,

in Your name,

and smile by smile,

hug by hug,

change the world.

When you can't put your prayers into words,
God hears your heart.

UNKNOWN

The Lord is the everlasting God, the Creator of the ends of the
earth. He does not faint or grow weary;
his understanding is unsearchable. He gives power
to the faint, and strengthens the powerless.
Even youths will faint and be weary,
and the young will fall exhausted;
but those who wait for the Lord
shall renew their strength,
they shall mount up with wings like eagles,
they shall run and not be weary,
they shall walk and not faint.

ISAIAH 40:28–31 (NRSV)

STILLNESS

five

STILLNESS

During my days of deepest grief, in all of my shock,
sorrow and struggle, I sat at the feet of God.
I literally spent hours each day reading God's word,
meditating on scripture and praying.
I intentionally spent a significant amount of time
being still before God.

RICK WARREN

AFTER THE SUCCESS of The Bible series on the History channel, Mark and I had the chance to do a follow-up series for NBC called *A.D.: The Bible Continues.* By this time, we had only one child left at home, Cameron, who was in his last year of high school. James and Reilly were both off at college in Boston. This kind of series can require a lot of travel and the need to be gone for long periods of time. Cameron, who had dreams of going to film school when he graduated, decided to take a semester off to come with us to Morocco and work on the crew. Mark and I were thrilled. We loved that we would be able to provide this incredible learning opportunity for Cameron, and we loved that we'd have him with us during the long months on location.

But just a few weeks into filming, Cameron got incredibly sick. At first we thought it was food poisoning, which can happen in foreign countries where the food and water are quite different from that in the States. Simultaneously, we were also filming a series in Malta called *The Dovekeepers* for CBS, so we took him with us to Malta, hoping that the change in diet might help. At first, much to our relief, he seemed to improve, but after a few days, it became clear that it was a much more serious issue than food poisoning, and he was admitted to the hospital.

Mark and I waited anxiously, holding each other close and praying, as the doctor examined him. We just wanted him to be okay. Cameron was very brave, and though we tried to appear strong in front of him, we were incredibly worried. After scans and tests and hushed conversations, the doctor finally pulled us aside to share his diagnosis.

Cameron had a brain tumor. Our hearts sank. But the doctor returned with what he promised was good news. The tu-

Do not worry about anything, but in everything by prayer and supplication with thanksgiving let your requests be made known to God. And the peace of God, which surpasses all understanding, will guard your hearts and your minds in Christ Jesus.

PHILIPPIANS 4:6–7 (NRSV)

mor was operable. He advised we get Cameron back to the States and have surgery performed as soon as possible.

Mark immediately arranged a plane for a medical evacuation from the location, and an ambulance was waiting in Los Angeles to take Cameron straight to the hospital.

And thus began a time that truly felt like the darkest of days, where all that we had taken for granted was now held in the hands of God. Of course, it had all been in His hands before, but now we acutely felt the reality that we had no power over the situation.

It was a frightening time for all of us, and we found ourselves clinging to hope but ultimately having to surrender to God.

Here we were at the peak of our careers. The Bible series had been a huge success; our company, LightWorkers Media, had just merged with MGM; and we were filming two network shows at the same time. But this incident with our son brought us to our knees, literally. None of that success mattered; we would have traded it all just to have Cameron completely well again.

We were so grateful to have access to the very best care and a fantastic team of doctors at UCLA Medical Center. But Cameron's issues were complicated, and we immediately called in prayers. We reached out to friends and family and our church community all across the country, knowing that we needed a miracle. We needed Cameron to be covered in prayer. We didn't know what would happen, but we knew we needed God. Both for his healing and for strength for our family to withstand these days.

Mark and I are both producers. In our day-to-day lives, members of the cast or crew come to us with situations that need fixing, and we help to figure things out. We help solve problems. But the situation with Cameron was filled with unknowing and uncertainty. We felt powerless to solve this "problem." There was nothing to be done except to call on God.

Mark was an absolute pillar of strength in this crisis. He is a natural leader, and he moved to make the smartest medical choices on behalf of Cameron. I can honestly say that if you were hanging off a cliff on the end of a rope, you would want Mark Burnett on the other end. He never gives up and he never lets go. He is completely loving and reliable and dependable. He stepped into this situation, taking whatever actions were needed, holding tightly to his boy, and he never let go. With no quick fix in sight, it became a waiting game, and we soon knew we would be at the hospital for some time. At the nurse's suggestion, we decided to take shifts to give each other a break to get home to have a quick shower or grab a change of clothes. The hospital told us we were in this for the long haul, and we had to be smart or we would not endure.

> There is no pit so deep that God's love is not deeper still.
>
> CORRIE TEN BOOM

Before we left for Morocco, we had started some renovations at our home, thinking it was the perfect time, as we

The Lord will fight for you, you need only to be still.

EXODUS 14:14 (NIV)

would be gone and out of the country for several months. Now we were unexpectedly back, and our house was in chaos. It was a shock to walk in and discover walls removed, plastic sheeting all over the place, and a coating of dust everywhere.

We have always called our home "the Sanctuary," and if ever we needed a space of peace and calm, it was now. We needed a sanctuary, but with builders in the house, we certainly weren't going to find it at home. We thought about checking into a hotel, but ultimately decided we still wanted the comfort and security that comes from being in your own home and being able to crawl into your own bed. We would deal with the chaos. The physical mess in our home was an outer reflection of what was going on in our emotional and spiritual lives.

Looking back, I see this time of our lives as a blur. We were all barely coping, in survival mode, and acting on pure instinct. Friends and family flew in from the UK to be of support. Of course Cameron's mother and her family were there, and James and Reilly flew home from college on the East Coast as often as they could to be at the hospital as well. James was such a great big brother, sitting for hours at his brother's bedside, holding his hand and refusing to leave even for a moment. It was a time of great worry for our little family, but looking back, I can see that it brought us all closer together, as we leaned on one another for support and strength.

I remember driving back and forth from the hospital, and those times alone in the car provided my most intimate moments with God. There were times I had to pull over on the side of the road and sit in the quiet of my car, weeping and listening for His still, small voice. There was no real peace at the hospital, where I tried to remain strong and be a good partner for Mark, and there was no stillness in our home with all the construction going on. Only in the privacy of my car could my soul allow itself to feel. *God, please heal him. Please, Lord, please, please heal him.* It was here, alone, where I could finally cry out to God and try to find the stillness within myself.

Prayer is a lifeline to God.
REV. BILLY GRAHAM

Days became weeks, and the worry was taking its toll. Mark, who stood watch over his son like a warrior angel morning, noon, and night, was just about worn out. Indeed, we all were exhausted. We were practically living at the hospital, and the uncertainty was frightening. When our dear friends Pastor Rick and Kay Warren came by and prayed with us and prayed over Cameron, it was not only a blessing to Cameron but it lifted our spirits as well.

Indeed, we were so grateful to all the friends who rallied around us—those who visited and those who reached out to us on email or on the phone, and we were particularly grateful to all those who reached out to us in prayer. We could feel the love that

Worry does not empty tomorrow of its sorrow, it empties today of its strength.

CORRIE TEN BOOM

surrounded us, and we were uplifted and strengthened by it. The whole experience had brought us to our knees. For in the fear and uncertainty, there was nowhere else to go but to God.

We cried out in our darkness and despair, and, mercifully, the Lord heard us. Cameron began to slowly recover.

Once we knew he was out of the woods and we had all breathed a sigh of relief together and cried tears of gratitude, I went out to my car and was finally alone, about to drive home to the Sanctuary. I fell to my knees in the parking lot. *Thank you, God. Thank you, God. Thank you, God.*

I'm not sure if I said the words, but I know God felt my prayer of gratitude through the tears that were streaming down my face.

In the midst of the crisis, there was a moment when we did not know if Cameron would ever walk or talk again, and yet when he was released from the hospital in time for an incredible Thanksgiving feast, he practically ran through our front door with a giant smile on his face. Healed and restored, talking a mile a minute. There was no doubt what we were all thankful for that year. We held hands tightly around our table and prayed together, thanking God for healing

Cameron, for giving him back his health, and for returning him to his loving family.

In many ways, the experience brought our little family closer together, which is an additional blessing. We no longer take each other or anything in our lives for granted. Our three wonderful children are all now young adults, making their way in the world, reaching for their dreams. We love them so much and are proud of each one of them. We are very close, and we try to gather as often as we can as a family, sharing laughter and love and food and conversation around the dining table. We always take time to give thanks and pray together before every meal, a

You don't choose your family. They are God's gift to you, as you are to them.
DESMOND TUTU

practice we began with our children when they were very young. Our hearts are full of gratitude for all our blessings and each other.

Prayer can mean so many things. It is most definitely the crying out to God for help. In those dark days of uncertainty, all I could do was simply call out, *Help him, God, heal him, God*. I feel certain God welcomed those prayers. I believe He welcomes us anytime we come to him, even if we have no words.

But prayer is more than asking. It is a conversation with our Beloved. It is a quieting of the soul, so we can hear. It is a stilling of the chaos, so we can see how God is all around us, if we only take the time to notice.

The bond that links your true family is not one of blood, but of respect and joy in each other's life.

RICHARD BACH

We are a nation of doers. Rather than human beings, we are human do-ings. We work and strive and talk and move and go, go, go.

But if we want to be at peace, we must stop.

Stop our working. Stop our talking. Stop even our praying.

Breathe in, breathe out.

Make space. Listen to the whispers of our hearts.

It is only in the quietness, in the stillness, that we can hear the voice of God.

Prayer is as natural an expression of faith as breathing is of life.

JONATHAN EDWARDS

Therefore I tell you, do not worry about your life, what you will eat or drink; or about your body, what you will wear. Is not life more than food, and the body more than clothes? Look at the birds of the air; they do not sow or reap or store away in barns, and yet your heavenly Father feeds them. Are you not much more valuable than they? Can any one of you by worrying add a single hour to your life?

And why do you worry about clothes? See how the flowers of the field grow. They do not labor or spin. Yet I tell you that not even Solomon in all his splendor was dressed like one of these. If that is how God clothes the grass of the field, which is here today and tomorrow is thrown into the fire, will he not much more clothe you—you of little faith? So do not worry, saying, 'What shall we eat?' or 'What shall we drink?' or 'What shall we wear?' For the pagans run after all these things, and your heavenly Father knows that you need them. But seek first his kingdom and his righteousness, and all these things will be given to you as well. Therefore do not worry about tomorrow, for tomorrow will worry about itself. Each day has enough trouble of its own.

Matthew 6:25-34 (NIV)

Praying

It doesn't have to be

the blue iris, it could be

weeds in a vacant lot, or a few

small stones; just

pay attention, then patch

a few words together and don't try

to make them elaborate, this isn't

a contest but the doorway

into thanks, and a silence in which

another voice may speak.

Mary Oliver

A SPACE FOR GRACE

You cannot in one glance survey this most vast and beautiful system of the universe, in its wide expanse, without being completely overwhelmed by the boundless force of its brightness.

JOHN CALVIN

When life begins to get messy and chaotic and loud, I have to take time away. I have to find a moment of stillness. And I find that stillness through prayer and in nature.

When I was growing up, we of course learned the Our Father, and I remember getting on my knees with my father and praying that prayer. And how important that prayer is. It is how Jesus Himself taught us to pray. But prayer can be much more than words that we say to God. T. S. Eliot says, "If we really want to pray, we must first learn to listen, for in the silence of our hearts God speaks."

We are sometimes too busy to notice that God is trying to speak to us.

*May we all grow in grace and peace,
and not neglect the silence that is printed
in the centre of our being.
It will not fail us.*

THOMAS MERTON

Our culture is bombarded on all sides by demands. We live in a noisy world, with texting and emailing and music and TV and on and on. We used to be able to get away and have space . . . on the weekend, on a plane, at dinner. But now we are expected to be available at all times. To respond immediately.

It is only when we slow down that we are able to breathe. To connect with the spirit of God. To *hear* God. It is only in that peace that we can see the butterfly and notice the miracles unfolding all around. When we are still, we can get out of the way.

Stillness brings you into the present moment. We are often so fixated on something that happened in the past or worried about what might happen in the future that we completely miss the now.

Prayer can involve a time that you set aside to commune with God, but I like to try to bring prayer into every moment.

To call Him in, to invite Him into each moment. I feel this the strongest when I'm in nature. When we are surrounded by nature, we can finally commune with God and His creation. Walking out into a field or looking up at the sky allows us to breathe and recharge and reminds us how big our God is.

God is also in the small things. The song of a bird, the feel of the sun on

Yesterday is history. Tomorrow is a mystery. Today is a gift. That's why it's called the present.

ALICE MORSE EARLE

our skin, the buzz of the bumblebee, the flight of the butterfly. In every blade of grass we can see the beauty of creation.

In every walk with Nature one receives far more than he seeks.

JOHN MUIR

And there, in that space, we will find God.

I try to get out in nature each morning, either with a brisk hike along the mountain trails near our home or a quiet stroll on the beach. For you, it might mean walking your dog in your neighborhood or stepping out onto your porch and looking up at the sky. Spending time outside allows us to make space in our hearts for God. It gives us a chance to fill up, to nurture our souls so we can go into our day feeling in tune with what truly matters. No matter what you think about meditation, there is something to be said for developing the skill to quiet your mind. Whether you say the Rosary, simply count your breaths, or call out to God, meditation frees your mind of the noise and chatter; it gets you into a space of openness and availability.

This is one of the reasons I love living by the ocean. The constant sound of the waves becomes a meditation, washing in and out, as steady and consistent as my heartbeat, like a massage for my mind and my spirit.

I've also created rituals for myself throughout the day that allow me to stop and find stillness. Of course, since I am an Irishwoman, a cup of tea is the solution to everything! For in the process of making tea, there is space, there is waiting, there is quiet. There is ritual. First, you put water in the kettle, and then you wait for it to boil. Then you warm the pot, then put the tea in, pour in the boiling water, and wait for the tea to brew. By the time you sit down to your steaming cup of tea, all is well in the world. You have created what I like to call a "space for grace." Every moment in my past, big or small in memory, involved a cup of tea.

I See His Blood upon the Rose

I see his blood upon the rose
And in the stars the glory of his eyes,
His body gleams amid eternal snows,
His tears fall from the skies.

I see his face in every flower;
The thunder and the singing of the birds
Are but his voice—and carven by his power
Rocks are his written words.

All pathways by his feet are worn,
His strong heart stirs the ever-beating sea,
His crown of thorns is twined with every thorn,
His cross is every tree.

Joseph Mary Plunkett

You can find this space for grace anywhere, in any moment. When you go outside and look at the sky, when you read a book of poetry, or when you turn on a piece of music that you know stirs your soul. These are tools that can create in you a feeling of well-being and connect you with the spiritual

When anxious, uneasy and bad thoughts come, I go to the sea, and the sea drowns them out with its great wide sounds, cleanses me with its noise, and imposes a rhythm upon everything in me that is bewildered and confused.

RAINER MARIA RILKE

and with God. And, of course, reading the Bible and spending time in the Word of God is the ultimate way to invite Him into your heart and into each moment.

We have to remember to take care of ourselves, to slow down, and to nurture our relationship with God. Building a relationship with God is like building any other relationship. While God never stops loving us, we can feel disconnected from Him if we don't make space for Him, if we don't take the time to be quiet, to still the chatter and make room for His thoughts and His grace.

There are so many rituals from across different cultures that share the same intention, and those rituals can help us stop and remember and bring Him in. Whether they are performing the sign of the cross, splashing holy water, or lighting a candle as you make your prayer. These are all designed as gentle reminders. I have candles scattered throughout my house, and I light them wherever I go. For me, there is something about the scratch of the match against the carbon and the *whish* that comes when the flame bursts to light that ushers in the holy.

I have heard it said that we either live our lives as if nothing is a miracle or as if everything is a miracle. I, of course, believe that everything is a miracle, from the healing power of God to the stunning beauty of creation to the magical emotion that comes from a particular piece of music.

I strive to live each day making room to recognize these miracles and thank God for them. When you do that, you realize how close He is. That He is always right there, waiting for you, in your heart and mind. In times when you feel close to Him, and even times when you feel desperately far away, He is always there, waiting for you to call on Him.

Look within.

Look without.

He is there.

Faith is the bird that feels the light
when the dawn is still dark.

RABINDRANATH TAGORE

In the middle of sentences loaded with action—healing suffering people, casting out devils, responding to impatient disciples, traveling from town to town and preaching from synagogue to synagogue—we find these quiet words: "In the morning, long before dawn, he got up and left the house, and went off to a lonely place and prayed there." In the center of breathless activities, we hear a restful breathing. Surrounded by hours of moving, we find a moment of quiet stillness. In the heart of much involvement, there are words of withdrawal. In the midst of action, there is contemplation. And after much togetherness, there is solitude. The more I read this nearly silent sentence locked in between the loud words of action, the more I have the sense that the secret of Jesus' ministry is hidden in that lonely place where he went to pray, early in the morning, long before dawn.

Henri Nouwen

In our lives in the world, the temptation is always to go where the world takes us, to drift with whatever current happens to be running strongest. When good things happen, we rise to heaven; when bad things happen, we descend to hell. When the world strikes out at us, we strike back, and when one way or another the world blesses us, our spirits soar. I know this to be true of no one as well as I know it to be true of myself. I know how just the weather can affect my whole state of mind for good or ill, how just getting stuck in a traffic jam can ruin an afternoon that in every other way is so beautiful that it dazzles the heart. We are in constant danger of being not actors in the drama of our own lives but reactors. The fragmentary nature of our experience shatters us into fragments. Instead of being whole, most of the time we are in pieces, and we see the world in pieces, full of darkness at one moment and full of light the next.

It is in Jesus, of course, and in the people whose lives have been deeply touched by Jesus, and in ourselves at those moments when we also are deeply touched by him, that we see another way of being human in this world, which is the way of wholeness. When we glimpse that wholeness in others, we recognize it immediately for what it is, and the reason we recognize it, I believe, is that no matter how much the world shatters us to pieces, we carry inside us a *vision* of wholeness that we sense is our true home and that beckons to us. It is part of what the book of Genesis means by saying that we are made in the image of God.

Frederick Buechner

Today

Today I'm flying low and I'm

not saying a word.

I'm letting all the voodoos of ambition sleep.

The world goes on as it must,

the bees in the garden rumbling a little,

the fish leaping, the gnats getting eaten.

And so forth.

But I'm taking the day off.

Quiet as a feather.

I hardly move though really I'm traveling

a terrific distance.

Stillness. One of the doors

into the temple.

Mary Oliver

The Lake Isle of Innisfree

I will arise and go now, and go to Innisfree,
And a small cabin build there, of clay and wattles made:
Nine bean-rows will I have there, a hive for the honey-bee,
And live alone in the bee-loud glade.

And I shall have some peace there, for peace comes dropping
    slow,
Dropping from the veils of the morning to where the cricket
    sings;
There midnight's all a glimmer, and noon a purple glow,
And evening full of the linnet's wings.

I will arise and go now, for always night and day
I hear lake water lapping with low sounds by the shore;
While I stand on the roadway, or on the pavements grey,
I hear it in the deep heart's core.

William Butler Yeats

THE FIELD

O Beauty, you are the light of the world!

DEREK WALCOTT

My father had a quiet stillness about him. When we would go to Moville in the summers, my father loved to walk along the shore at Greencastle. We would walk along that rocky seashore, me beside him, in complete easy silence, sometimes for hours.

Many years later, I finally had a bit of money saved after the success of *A Woman Named Jackie*. I still didn't own a car or a home in the U.S., yet I had this idea that maybe I would buy a wee cottage in Ireland, a little corner for myself in the world. I looked around at some different towns but didn't find anything I liked. I soon found myself back in Greencastle, and there, along the very shore that I used to walk with Dad, was a small field for sale. Now, there was no cottage on it. Just a field. I had no idea or real plan for what I was going to do with a field. But I wanted that field. I wanted that field for my dad.

In a matter of days, I was signing the contract with the

village solicitor. And then I took my rented car and drove out to what was now my field. It had been raining earlier, and so I had my Wel-

> *Out beyond ideas of wrongdoing and rightdoing, there is a field. I will meet you there.*
>
> RUMI

lington boots on, and the ground was still damp and muddy. I climbed the fence and went and sat in the middle of the field, staring out at the waters of Lough Foyle. And I laughed and cried, thinking, *Fine lot of good this old field is going to do me!*

But then the breeze blew, and I'm sure I felt my dad's hand on my shoulder. And I imagined him saying, "Aren't you a great girl, now. Good on ya."

And I smiled. I had bought this field for my dad. And I knew wherever he was, he was pleased. He would have just loved it, of that I am certain.

I kept that field for many years.

And yes, I can see that it was a very impractical purchase. I still laugh to think that the very first thing I bought with the money I earned was a field for my dead father. But we all so want our parents to be proud of us. He wasn't around to see what I had done, to see the life I was creating for myself. I bought that field as if to say, *See, Dad, look what I did!*

And I know I felt his pride in that field that day.

To me, a field can be just as holy as the largest cathedral. It can usher in a moment just as profound as the greatest sermon.

You see, the holy is everywhere. It is in the sun and the moon and the stars. It is in you and me. We often go looking for it. We think we will be able to find space on vacation or when we go to church. We are always waiting. When we get there, then we will be happy or whole or complete. But it is here. Already here. In you and in me.

We just have to stop, and breathe, and listen. And see that it has been in us all along.

What wings are to a bird, and sails to a ship,
so is prayer to the soul.

CORRIE TEN BOOM

Lord, you have been our dwelling place

throughout all generations.

Before the mountains were born

or you brought forth the whole world,

from everlasting to everlasting

you are God.

Psalm 90: 1-2 (NIV)

I know, God, that you are only
as far away as my next breath.
That you are always there, waiting, in
the stillness inside,
if only I would stop and find you.
Thank you for the reminders you put
in our lives.
To slow down.
To breathe. To wonder.
Thank you for the ocean,
that magnificent display
of your glory
and your power.
Thank you for the sun
that warms our skin,
for the breeze that
makes our hair dance,
for the flowers that
not only delight our eyes
but tickle our noses
with their delicious scent.
You have made our world
a wonder of beauty.
Thank you.
Thank you for reminders,
for stillness,
for grace.

If there is light in the soul, there will be beauty in the person. If there is beauty in the person, there will be harmony in the house. If there is harmony in the house, there will be order in the nation. If there is order in the nation, there will be peace in the world.

CHINESE PROVERB

Everything is possible for one who believes.

MARK 9:23 (NIV)

GRATITUDE

six

GRATITUDE

I wouldn't have dared ask God for all He has given me.
I couldn't have done it on my own.
I thank God every day for what I have.

LORETTA LYNN

IT ALL COMES down to one thing: gratitude.

Every morning when I get out of bed and my first foot hits the floor, I say, "Thank." Then the other foot hits the floor, and I say, "You." And all the way into the bathroom, I am whispering, "Thank you. Thank you. Thank you." A pitter-patter of gratitude as I begin my day.

I began this practice when I was filming *Touched by an Angel* in Utah. I don't remember where I read or heard about it, but as soon as I discovered this practice, I knew it was something I wanted to integrate into my daily routine. And I've done it every day ever since.

I've now added another routine to remind me to give thanks

throughout the day. Each time I wash my hands and feel the water run over my skin, I say it again. "Thank you. Thank you, God." It helps me take a step back from whatever is happening in my day to remember my blessings. It's a reminder for me to acknowledge God; and from that space, I am brought into a place of strength and wholeness and fullness. I find when I attach an attitude to an action—something I am bound to do throughout the day—it helps me remember the attitude more. And so every time I wash my hands, my perception of whatever is going on around me instantly changes.

I think that practice spoke to me while I was in Utah because I was so grateful during that season of my life. So grateful to be cast in a starring role on a TV show, so thankful that the series had been picked up and that it had finally found its audience. While *Touched by an Angel* eventually went on to become the number one show on the network, the first year or two it really struggled to find its audience. We shot the pilot not knowing if it would be picked up, and CBS initially ordered only six episodes, then increased it to thirteen. They kept moving our time slot, and we were even placed on an early hiatus for a while—which often signals that the end is in sight and that the show will be canceled. But then, finally, they put us in a Saturday-night time slot, and we began to pick up some ratings. We realized, as a cast and crew, that if we didn't do something to spread the word, this show would be over before it even had a chance to begin, which often happens. So we reached out to youth groups and churches all across the country and let them know that there was a TV show on the air that celebrated God and was hoping to spread the message of God's love. And slowly the faith community began to mobilize, word of

One more day to serve.
One more hour to love.
One more minute to praise.
For this day I am grateful.
If I awaken to the morning sun,
I am grateful.

MARY LOU KOWNACKI,
ORDER OF SAINT BENEDICT

mouth began to spread, the churches began to pray, and we became the little engine that could. *I think I can, I think I can, I think I can.*

Finally, the network moved us to Sunday night. That was the sweet spot. Families could gather at the end of the weekend to watch this show together. Parents and grandparents could snuggle on the couch with their kids and know they didn't have to keep their finger on the remote control. They trusted the show and enjoyed the message of hope. Soon millions of people were watching each week.

Talk about gratitude. It was more than any of us could have hoped for.

And we soon realized that it was more than entertainment; we came to believe that God was truly using our show to reach His children.

I was so moved by letters I received from people who shared how a particular episode impacted them and deeply touched their lives. Because I was the face of the show, many of these letters were addressed to me, but I would bring them to set to share with my cast and crew. We would laugh and cry and hug, hearing the messages from these viewers, so grateful for the opportunity to be part of something that was clearly bigger than all of us. As Della would say, "It's a God thing, baby."

One time I was at a bookstore in Los Angeles doing a signing for a children's book I had written, and a young woman came up to me, tears in her eyes and fresh scars on her wrists. And she told me the most remarkable story.

She hadn't had an easy life, and one night she found herself full of despair and ready to take her own life. She slit her wrists and slid down the bathroom wall, filled with anger at her family because she felt abandoned and alone, feelings that had plagued her throughout her life. And now here she was, feeling abandoned and alone again. She cried out to God, "Even now, there's no one here! There's no one here." And she let her head sink to her knees, waiting for death to take her.

But then she heard something from the living room. It was the television. She didn't even remember turning it on. *Touched by an Angel* was on, and it was the angel revelation scene. And this woman heard the words of Monica the angel come wafting through the bathroom door: "You are not alone. You are never alone. Don't you know that God loves you?"

I am the light of the world. Whoever follows me will not walk in darkness, but will have the light of life.

JOHN 8:12 (ESV)

When she heard those words, she lifted her head. She felt those words were just for her. And she picked up a towel and wrapped up her wrists and called an ambulance.

I stared at her in shock and gave her a hug, tears flooding my eyes, and all I could say was, "Thank you, God."

Thank you, God.

Over and over. I was so humbled by what God was able to accomplish with that little show of ours.

God is willing and able to use any of us to do His work. We just have to be ready. How do you prepare yourself to be God's angel? We've touched on it throughout this book. You slow down so you can hear His whisper. Find the stillness. You look for ways to perform small acts of kindness. You dare to do something courageous and step out onto that water. You look for ways to love. For that's who and what God is. Love. You want to be His angel? Spread love.

Love.

Love.

After the show wrapped, I went through a time of mourning. I missed my cast and crew family, but I also missed Monica. I missed playing her and inhabiting her spirit. Playing Monica for many hours a day, over many years, taught me so much. She made me a better friend, a better listener, a more faithful servant. I enjoyed living in her skin, and I think she brought out the best of me. She was able to truly, fully show up for someone. She listened, not just with her ears but also with her heart. When people come to you with a heart-load of hurt, they aren't always looking for solutions or answers. It's often enough just to listen and love. When people feel they are truly heard, healing can happen.

I also missed the important work we were doing, the purpose that I felt in my life. Reilly and I had come back to Malibu, and I wasn't sure what I was going to do next; but I knew I didn't want to just jump into another role.

One of the first things I filmed after the show wrapped was an infomercial for Operation Smile, a short film to increase awareness of the good work that they do. I had been meaning to do it ever since I had gotten involved with this wonderful organization after the first season of the show, but I hadn't had enough time to go on location to shoot it. So I packed my bags and headed off to Vietnam. I spent a week at the mission hospital, working to tell the story of children whose lives had been forever changed with this restorative surgery. I was grateful to be able to help bring attention to the cause and to help raise millions of dollars for this organization that brings so much hope and light into the world.

After that, I just waited. I waited, knowing that God would bring forth the right next step for me. I poured myself into being a mom. I loved being there for Reilly in a way I hadn't been able to do when I was putting in twelve-hour days on set. A number of job opportunities presented themselves, but I kept waiting. I didn't want to say yes to something out of fear of becoming irrelevant. If a job wasn't going to bring light and hope, I wasn't that interested.

But I had been chasing work for my entire life. It was scary to not work. I had to trust that space, even when waves of panic came crashing in.

The Bible says there is a time for everything. A time for sowing and reaping. Even Jesus took time to be alone and away from the crowds, time to pray, to gather Himself, before he went back out to do the good work.

I had no idea at the time that the next big thing for me would be the *Bible* project, but of course Mark had to come into my life before that could come to fruition.

I'm so thankful that God gave me the courage to wait. For Mark. For the Bible series. For Him.

Many people are surprised that my husband and I are able to work together. I have girlfriends who joke that they can hardly wash dishes with their husbands without getting into a disagreement! But I know God brought Mark and me together for a greater purpose. I often tell people that he and I have different skill sets and that we are quite a team when put together. Sometimes, to get a project made, you need to kick down a door; and there is no better man to kick a door down than my husband! But sometimes the door requires a gentle knock, and that's what I am able to do. Either way, the doors opened for us together. Our production company is named LightWorkers Media, and we believe it's better to light one candle than to curse the darkness.

Thank you, God. For my beautiful family. Thank you for my husband, Mark. For the important work you are guiding us to do together. Thank you for helping us find a way to bring your light into the world in an industry that isn't always interested in the light.

Sometimes it feels as if there is so much darkness in the world. I want to be a helper to bring people to the light. To spread the light. To shine the light. God is the Light, and He is always there.

Oh, there were many times when I was not as patient as I sound now. There were times when I would call out to Monica and say, somewhat jokingly, "Where are you when I need you? I miss you!"

> I don't think of all the misery, but of the beauty that still remains.
>
> ANNE FRANK

But of course, she *was* there, wasn't she? The angel is just the conduit of spirit. And in those moments, those moments when I was laughing as I called on Monica, I was calling out to God. And I would feel Him come alongside me, just as He came alongside those footprints in the sand, and say, *I'm right here, it's okay. Just sit. You don't have to be doing all the time. Just trust. You are doing enough.*

You are not alone. I'm right here with you.

Thank you, God.

There are two ways of spreading light: to be the candle or the mirror that reflects it.

EDITH WHARTON

*If the only prayer you said
in your whole life was "thank you,"
that would suffice.*

MEISTER ECKHART

STOP LOOKING FOR LACK

Acceptance doesn't mean resignation; it means
understanding that something is what it is
and that there's got to be a way through it.

MICHAEL J. FOX

I've learned one thing from being in this industry for almost thirty years now. Theodore Roosevelt probably said it best: "Comparison is the thief of joy." No matter what you have accomplished, there will always be someone with "more." More awards, more work, longer legs, bigger house. Trust me, the list can go on and on. I have more than I could have ever imagined in my wildest dreams, and yet there are still people with way more than me, if I choose to live my life in comparison.

That's why gratitude is so essential. There is no room for comparison within the words "Thank you." Thank you is fullness. Thank you is overflowing. Thank you is blessed beyond measure. There is no lack; there is only abundance. That's why we must learn to say thank you all the time. For every gift, big or small. For a home to live in, a job that pays the bills, a person to love, a child to raise. Saying thank you not only acknowledges all we've been given but also makes room for more to arrive.

To lift up the hands in prayer gives God glory, but a man with a dungfork in his hand, a woman with a slop pail, give Him glory, too. God is so great that all things give Him glory if you mean that they should.

GERARD MANLEY HOPKINS

I find that when I live with an "attitude of gratitude," I am attuned to the blessings of God. I am always looking for the next gift He might bestow, the next butterfly that will encourage me, the next quiet whisper of His voice.

When I am focused on what I don't have, I miss the blessings all around.

Perhaps you've heard the story of God's lifeboat. I'm not sure who wrote it, but it's become a kind of epistle of the many ways we can miss God.

As the story goes, there was a huge storm, and the emergency personnel sent a warning to the community that a flood was likely. They encouraged people to evacuate to keep themselves safe.

And a man said to himself: *I trust God and know that He will send a miracle to save me.*

His neighbors came by and said, "We are leaving, and there is room for you in our car. Please, come with us!"

But the man said, "No, I know that God will save me."

A few hours later, as the waters continued to rise, now licking at his front porch, a man in a canoe paddled over to his porch. "The waters are rising quickly. Come into my canoe, and I will get you to safety!"

But the man said, "No, thank you, God will save me."

A few hours later, the water had entered the house, and the man had to go up to his second story. A police boat arrived. The police saw him through his window, and said, "Come on, get in before it's too late!"

But again the man refused, saying, "No, thank you, God will save me."

By this time, the waters had reached the second floor, and the man had to climb onto his roof.

A helicopter was searching the area and found this lone man sitting on top of his roof as the sunset glimmered and darkness threatened.

"Sir, here is a rope, take hold, and we will pull you up and take you to safety!"

And sure enough, the man refused. "No, God will save me."

The waters continued to rise, and the man was washed away and drowned.

When he reached heaven, he walked up to God and said, accusingly, "God, I put my faith in you! Why didn't you save me?"

And God looked at him and said, "I sent you a warning,

a car, a canoe, a boat, and a helicopter. What more were you looking for?"

It's a silly story, but I think one that can show the power of thank you. What if, instead of saying "No, thanks" to every miracle God provided, the man instead had said, "Thank you"? He would have been safe at the very beginning. He would have been filled with wonder at the way God provides. He would have been a part of the chorus singing God's praise.

"Thank you" changes everything.

There have been times in my life when I have been disappointed, when I didn't book a job I thought should have been mine, or when God didn't answer my prayer the way I expected.

It's not always easy. That's why simply saying thank you throughout the day attunes you to what is right—not what is wrong—and reminds you where God has shown up, rather than where He is missing.

You don't want to miss the boat, do you?

Christ with me, Christ before me, Christ behind me,

Christ in me, Christ beneath me, Christ above me,

Christ on my right, Christ on my left,

Christ where I lie, Christ where I sit, Christ where I arise,

Christ in the heart of every one who thinks of me,

Christ in the mouth of every one who speaks to me,

Christ in every eye that sees me,

Christ in every ear that hears me.

Salvation is of the Lord.

Salvation is of the Christ.

May your salvation, Lord, be ever with us.

Saint Patrick

A CAUSE FOR CELEBRATION

Find a place inside where there's joy, and the joy
will burn out the pain.

JOSEPH CAMPBELL

When I experienced great loss very early in my life, I could have let that loss define me. I might have felt justified to walk around with a chip on my shoulder, feeling as if life had dealt me a bad hand. Those losses could have shaken me to the core of who I am. But my father helped me to see the butterfly, remember? So early in my life, his example taught me to . . . look for the miracle.

Gratitude helps us see the light in the darkness, the potential of healing among the sick, the hope among the hopeless. In spite of what I've lost, I haven't lost everything. I know gratitude is the key. The key to everything.

When I'm out in nature . . . thank you.

When I see a butterfly . . . thank you.

When I see good people doing their best to make this world a better place . . . thank you.

Viktor Frankl, who experienced the horrors of the concentration camp, famously said, "Between stimulus and response, there is a space. In that space is our power to choose our response. In our response lies our growth and our freedom."

That someone who experienced one of the darkest moments of our human history can see hope still, gives me hope. He would not be defined by what happened to him. Instead he said: "Everything can be taken from man but one thing: the last of the human freedoms—to choose one's attitude in any given set of circumstances, to choose one's own way."

We can choose darkness and lack. Or we can choose light, hope, and gratitude.

May we all choose light.

My life has been geared toward a search for light, a desire to see the helpers, not just the helpless. Perhaps that has been why I've been so drawn to the work of Operation Smile. The people in this organization are bringers of light. They see the children in need of surgery; they see the hole that no one is filling. And they take time out of their busy lives to go and fill that hole. To heal that child. What they do truly changes lives. Those healed children go forth into their lives with a new call, a renewed hope, and a beam of light that shines brightly wherever they go. Those children know the call of gratitude. It is

Life is 10% what happens to you and 90% how you react to it.

CHARLES SWINDOLL

in their eyes, in their now-bright smiles, in their hugs and kisses.

Thank you. To the doctor who healed me. The person who donated. And God, who is the ultimate healer.

There is a parable that tells the story of a man walking on a beach covered with thousands of starfish. They literally litter the beach, making it hard to walk. And as the man gazes along the shore, he notices a little boy walking carefully through the starfish and every now and then stopping, gingerly picking up a starfish, and throwing it into the sea. The man walks up to the boy to ask him what he is doing. And the boy explains that when the tide goes out, all these starfish will die, no longer close to the sea, and unable to reach their home. The man knows this is true and says, "But there are too many out here for you to save. You won't really be able to make a difference."

The boy stops, picks up another starfish, and throws it into the water.

"It made a difference to that one," he says triumphantly.

No, we cannot save the entire world, but, one child at a time, we can make a difference. Let's not be paralyzed by the huge need in our world or overwhelmed by all the pain—and end up doing nothing. We must do *something*, and if we each do something, give something, help someone, then together we *can* make a difference.

In that way, we can live our lives as a chorus of gratitude.

There is no time to waste.

When I was growing up, we had a room that we called "the good room." It was the room where we would entertain guests, and in it lived a little china cabinet with glass doors, and within this was my mother's greatest treasure: a set of fine china that had been given to her as a wedding gift. Oh, how she loved that china. It was her most expensive and luxurious possession. As children, we were not often allowed in the good room, because she didn't want us playing in there and perhaps jostling the cabinet and breaking one of her precious dishes. The cabinet was locked with a little key, and my mother would only open it to wash the china, carefully dry it, and then arrange it back nicely inside.

One afternoon during the height of the Troubles, after the British army had arrived, we were all gathered in the kitchen. The army had brought these humongous armored Saracens that would rumble through our narrow streets. And when this happened, the entire house would shake.

This particular afternoon, we heard the telltale growl of a Saracen turning down our street, and then we began to feel the tremors as its large mass made its way up the hill. And as the house began to shake, we heard a loud crash come from the good room. My mother's hand flew to her face and she ran down the hallway, grabbing the key to the china cabinet as she went. But there was no need to open it. It was clear what had happened as soon as we walked into the room. The top shelf had collapsed onto the bottom shelf, and every single piece of her china was shattered.

My mother fell to her knees, opened the cabinet door, and cried, touching her precious china that was now destroyed for good.

You can cut all the flowers but you cannot keep Spring from coming.

PABLO NERUDA

That image has stayed with me for my entire life.

We all have things we want to save, that we want to preserve. But my mother was keeping that china for what? A special day sometime in the future? Sadly, she never got to enjoy it.

And I've learned from that to enjoy each moment for the blessing it is, because none of us is guaranteed anything more than right now.

I'm someone who wants to jump in and seize the moment. I'm not locking up any rooms. Let's thank God for every gift and use it to its fullest.

An attitude of gratitude means every day is the best. Every day is a cause for celebration. From the beauty of the sunrise to the splendor of the sunset, may we all bask in the glory that God has given.

Thank you, God.

Thank you, God.

Thank you, God.

There is treasure buried in the field of every one of our days, even the bleakest or dullest, and it is our business, as we journey, to keep our eyes peeled for it.

FREDERICK BUECHNER

The belief that *happiness has to be deserved* has led to centuries of pain, guilt, and deception. So firmly have we clung to this single, illusory belief that we've almost forgotten the real truth about happiness. So busy are we trying to *deserve* happiness that we no longer have much time for ideas such as: *Happiness is natural, happiness is a birthright, happiness is free, happiness is a choice, happiness is within,* and *happiness is being.* The moment you believe that happiness has to be deserved, you must toil for evermore.

Robert Holden

Thank
You,
God.

There's no place like home.

DOROTHY, *THE WIZARD OF OZ*

Praise be to the God and Father of our Lord Jesus Christ, who has blessed us in the heavenly realms with every spiritual blessing in Christ. For he chose us in him before the creation of the world to be holy and blameless in his sight. In love he predestined us for adoption to sonship through Jesus Christ, in accordance with his pleasure and will—to the praise of his glorious grace, which he has freely given us in the One he loves.

EPHESIANS 1:3-6 (NIV)

seven

HOME

*My soul is from elsewhere, I'm sure of that,
and I intend to end up there.*

Rumi

I KNOW THAT the reason I was able to keep going after the loss of my mother was that my faith had taught me I would see her again. My faith told me, *Yes, this hurts. Yes, life is hard. But take heart. This is not the end. Jesus rose after three days, and our spirits, too, are immortal. There is a place waiting for you. It is filled with God and your loved ones. All tears will be dried. All hurts will be healed. It is paradise, and it is forever.*

I'm not sure where I would be if I didn't have that hope as a guiding force in my life.

I found a Welsh word the other day that I had never come across before: *hiraeth.* It is defined as a homesickness for a home to which you cannot return, a home that maybe never was; the nostalgia, the yearning, the grief for the lost places of your past.

Of course I responded to that word as a girl whose childhood essentially ended at age ten when her mother's bright light was taken from this world. I do feel as if I've carried a longing for that home ever since . . . the home that was filled with laughter and joy and a mother's love.

But I also respond to the part of the definition that speaks of a home that maybe never was. Because this world is filled with longing. None of us have perfect lives. I can attest that all the money and success in the world doesn't fill our hearts. There is a void in each of us that I believe can only be filled by God and will only be fully healed when we reach heaven.

For all the gifts I've been given, I still long. I long for my mom and dad. I long for Reilly to meet her grandparents. I long to share stories with my parents of where life has taken me.

I long to feel that completeness of being with all of my loved ones together.

And I know I will have that in heaven. That not only will I be able to walk with my mom and dad again but one day, I hope many years after I've arrived, I will see my own baby girl walk through those gates. And I will embrace her. And then I will pull her over to my mother

> *Death is no more than passing from one room into another. But there's a difference for me, you know. Because in that other room I shall be able to see.*
>
> HELEN KELLER

and my father. And they will see their beautiful granddaughter. And we will hug and laugh and cry at the good and the bad and the love and the joy. And the grace that allowed us to finally be together, forever.

Billy Graham famously said, "My home is in heaven. I'm just passing through this world." Sometimes we search so hard to find home. We think we will find it in the perfect job or perfect relationship, or maybe if we build just the right house or move to the right neighborhood, everything will fall into place. But true home is within us. True home is in God. We're like Dorothy in *The Wizard of Oz*: she thinks she needs certain things to make her whole and get her back home. She thinks she needs courage and heart and a brain. She thinks that if she could just pull back the curtain and find Oz, all would be well. But when she gets back home, she realizes that what she truly needs has been with her all along.

> We shall not cease from exploration
> And the end of all our exploring
> Will be to arrive where we started
> And know the place for the first time.
>
> T. S. ELIOT

I hope that in this book you have begun to see the beauty in your journey. How it may have twisted and turned, and had ups and downs, but ultimately that you were never alone on the Yellow Brick Road. That even in the dark forest, God was preparing you. That even as you danced in Munchkinland, it was time to say *thank you.* That even though when you arrive back home and nothing has changed on the outside, you'll see that you've been changed on the inside. And that is all that matters. When we awaken fully to God, it's as if we finally remember that we are not merely caterpillars but that we are, in fact, beautiful butterflies with wings to fly.

Human spiritual longing is, finally,
the humility of realizing that we have forgotten
who we are. . . . There can be times in the process
of seeking that we are reassured that however
much we are searching, we are at some level
even more devoutly being searched for. There may even
be times when we are reassured that the
frenzy of searching is not really needed, that in
fact we have already been found. But the longing
will persist, and so will the seeking, and unless we
are unusually fortunate we shall search
in a multitude of blind alleys.

GERALD MAY

When We All Get to Heaven

Sing the wondrous love of Jesus,
Sing His mercy and His grace.
In the mansions bright and blessed
He'll prepare for us a place.

(Refrain)
When we all get to Heaven,
What a day of rejoicing that will be!
When we all see Jesus,
We'll sing and shout the victory!

While we walk the pilgrim pathway,
Clouds will overspread the sky;
But when trav'ling days are over,
Not a shadow, not a sigh.

Let us then be true and faithful,
Trusting, serving every day;
Just one glimpse of Him in glory
Will the toils of life repay.

Onward to the prize before us!
Soon His beauty we'll behold;
Soon the pearly gates will open;
We shall tread the streets of gold.

Eliza E. Hewitt

The Journey

Above the mountains
    the geese turn into
        the light again

painting their
    black silhouettes
        on an open sky.

Sometimes everything
    has to be
        inscribed across
        the heavens

so you can find
    the one line
        already written
        inside you.

Sometimes it takes
    a great sky
        to find that

first, bright
and indescribable
wedge of freedom
in your own heart.

Sometimes with
the bones of the black
sticks left when the fire
has gone out

someone has written
something new
in the ashes
of your life.

You are not leaving,
even as the light
fades quickly now,
you are arriving.

David Whyte

GOD'S CALLING CARD

See, I am sending an angel ahead of you to guard you along the way and to bring you to the place I have prepared.

EXODUS 23:20 (NIV)

I love the saying that some attribute to Albert Einstein: "Coincidence is God's way of remaining anonymous." I love to look for how beautiful things come together in a way that shows there was a plan, that there were greater forces at work. Either there is no God or there is only God. I, of course, strive to live my life believing that it is all God at work.

Sometimes you have to look for those "coincidences," and other times they are so obvious you can only laugh and thank God. These gifts, these simple moments that show that He is here and that your loved ones are still surrounding you, are the ones that lift my heart and give me strength. They show me that the veil between this world and the next is just that, a thin veil. We are closer than we think, though we may feel so far. Separation is just an illusion.

Several years ago, Mark and I hosted a table at an Operation Smile gala. I have been an ambassador for this wonderful organization for many years, and on this particular night we joined a group of friends all there to support this worthy cause. We were sitting down to dinner when a young girl came around the tables trying to sell raffle tickets. We had already donated, so my first impulse was to politely decline. But this girl was hovering around the table, and she reminded me a bit of Reilly, so I dug into my purse to see what cash I had. I had forty dollars, and the tickets were twenty dollars each, so I bought two tickets and wrote my name on them, and the girl moved on to the next table.

One of my dear friends, Brooke Burke-Charvet, was the MC for the night, and as dinner was wrapping up, she went up onstage with a very large hat filled with raffle tickets. And as she put her hand deep into that hat, she pulled out a ticket and said, "Well, it's my friend Roma Downey!"

I jumped up like I'd just won an Oscar. I'd never really won anything like this before and was so excited. Mark pulled me back to my chair, laughing, as there was nothing to go up and receive; you would find out later what the prize was.

It turned out that the prize was choosing a piece of jewelry from the designer Thanh Hoang. They gave Thanh my contact information, and a few weeks later I invited her out to my house to look at her beautiful jewelry collection and share some tea.

After Thanh arrived and we'd settled in for our tea, she reached into her bag and pulled out a few pieces of jewelry for me to choose from her collection, Le Dragon d'Or.

She sat there with her hand in her bag, and she looked me in the eye.

"Roma, I have one piece of jewelry I made about fifteen years ago. No one has ever bought it, so I have stopped showing it. It is an unusual piece. But as I was leaving this morning, I had a strong feeling I should bring it. You may not like it, which is fine—I have a few other pieces as well—but I wanted to show you this one first."

And she pulled out a beautiful butterfly ring.

Tears sprang to my eyes. Immediately, I knew it was from my mom. That it was a message from her. *I'm still here, Roma. All these years later, I'm still right here.*

Of course I chose that piece of jewelry. Nothing else would do. That ring was a gift from my dear mother. It was meant for me.

I later learned that when Brooke picked the second raffle ticket out of the hat, as there were two prizes to be won that night, my name was on the ticket again! But she, of course, put it aside. She couldn't have me winning both prizes; it might have looked rigged. What are the chances my name was pulled out twice?

But to me, that shows how much my mother wanted me to get her message. What are the odds? That I would end up buying a raffle ticket despite my initial resistance. That my name would be the one to be called, out of the hun-

Sometimes the heart sees what is invisible to the eye.

H. JACKSON BROWN JR.

dreds in that hat. Twice! And that unbeknownst to me, the prize would be a butterfly ring.

Those moments were so validating to me. I then understood that my mother is still reaching out to me. That I will see her again. That I will be reunited with the loving energy of my mom and dad, even though I don't know exactly what heaven may look like.

Now, some may say that it was just a coincidence that my name was called and that that designer felt called to bring a butterfly ring.

But I like to see those coincidences as signs of God's love, as reminders of his constant presence, and that I am truly a beloved child of God. And He is taking care of me in moments big and small.

For all who are led by the Spirit of God are sons of God. For you did not receive the spirit of slavery to fall back into fear, but you have received the Spirit of adoption as sons, by whom we cry, "Abba! Father!" The Spirit himself bears witness with our spirit that we are children of God, and if children, then heirs—heirs of God and fellow heirs with Christ, provided we suffer with him in order that we may also be glorified with him.

ROMANS 8:14–17 (ESV)

Late have I loved Thee, O Lord; and behold,
Thou wast within and I without, and there I sought Thee.
Thou was with me when I was not with Thee.
Thou didst call, and cry, and burst my deafness.
Thou didst gleam, and glow, and dispell my blindness.
Thou didst touch me, and I burned for Thy peace.
For Thyself Thou hast made us,
and restless our hearts until in Thee they find their ease.
Late have I loved Thee,
Thou Beauty ever old and ever new.
Thou hast burst my bonds asunder;
unto Thee will I offer up an offering of praise.

Saint Augustine

Danny Boy

Oh, Danny Boy, the pipes, the pipes are calling
From glen to glen, and down the mountainside;
The summer's gone, and all the roses falling
It's you, it's you must go and I must bide.

But come ye back when summer's in the meadow,
Or when the valley's hush'd and white with snow;
It's I'll be there in sunshine or in shadow,
Oh, Danny Boy, oh, Danny Boy, I love you so!

But when ye come, and all the flow'rs are dying
If I am dead, as dead I well may be,
Ye'll come and find the place where I am lying,
And kneel and say an Ave there for me.

And I shall hear, though soft you tread above me,
And all my grave will warmer, sweeter be,
For you will bend and tell me that you love me,
And I shall sleep in peace until you come to me!

Frederic Weatherly

THE REMEMBERING

Define yourself radically as one beloved by God.
This is the true self. Every other identity is illusion.

JOHN EAGAN

I hope that throughout this book you've come to remember: *We are all beloved children of God.*

No matter what you've done, no matter what mistakes you've made or pain you've caused, that truth doesn't change. We are His children. We are His beloved. There is nothing God won't do to bring us back to Him.

God shows us this in the Bible.

The Prodigal Son is not just a story to tell. It is our story.

Then Jesus said, "There was a man who had two sons. The younger of them said to his father, 'Father, give me the share of the property that will belong to me.' So he divided his property between them. A few days later the younger son gathered all he had and traveled to a distant country, and there he squandered his property in dissolute living. When he had spent everything, a severe famine took place throughout that coun-

try, and he began to be in need. So he went and hired himself out to one of the citizens of that country, who sent him to his fields to feed the pigs. He would gladly have filled himself with the pods that the pigs were eating; and no one gave him anything. But when he came to himself he said, 'How many of my father's hired hands have bread enough and to spare, but here I am dying of hunger! I will get up and go to my father, and I will say to him, "Father, I have sinned against heaven and before you; I am no longer worthy to be called your son; treat me like one of your hired hands."' So he set off and went to his father. But while he was still far off, his father saw him and was filled with compassion; he ran and put his arms around him and kissed him."

LUKE 15:11–20 (NRSV)

I am that son, and God is that Father. The Father who doesn't sit there shaking his head, wanting me to know the depth of my sin, but He is the Father who rejoices that I have come back and cannot wait for me to reach His door, and He comes running to envelop me in His arms. This is the kind of love God has for us. He doesn't reluctantly allow us back in; rather, He celebrates us and gives us robes and feasts and more than we could ever deserve.

We are His beloved.

My good friend and childhood parish priest Father Paddy O'Kane told me the following story: A young boy had been warned by his parents not to play with matches, and yet he was a curious boy and sneaked out to the barn with a box of matches to see how they worked. He loved the sound of the match striking, the smell of the sulfur as the match burst into flame, and, most of all, seeing the small flame glow. After a few minutes of this thrill, he accidently dropped one of the flaming matches, and the straw underfoot caught fire. He tried to stamp it out, but it caught too quickly, and before he knew it the floor was covered in flames. The boy ran out and looked on in horror as the entire barn was soon engulfed. Knowing that he was responsible, the boy ran out into the tall grass and hid, watching in shame as the entire barn burned to the ground.

When he saw his parents emerge from the house, he stayed hidden. He knew he had let them down and they would be angry. He watched as the fire engines arrived along with friends and neighbors. He saw his parents crying, and he knew they were so upset. And it was his fault.

The boy stayed hidden, even as night fell, afraid to confront his parents. *They must be so mad at me*, he thought.

But soon the night began to get very cold, and he was so hungry. He quietly walked up to the house and sneaked in the back door, hanging his head in shame.

*But when the set time had fully come, God sent his Son, born of a woman, born under the law, to redeem those under the law, that we might receive adoption to sonship. Because you are his sons, God sent the Spirit of his Son into our hearts, the Spirit who calls out, "**Abba**, Father." So you are no longer a slave, but God's child; and since you are his child, God has made you also an heir.*

GALATIANS 4:4–7 (NIV)

When his father saw him, he gasped.

"I'm so sorry, Daddy," the wee boy said.

And his father ran over to him and swept him up in a hug, kissing him, calling out to his wife, tears streaming down his face.

"Oh, my boy, my boy, we thought you were dead," the father whispered into his ear. "Thank you, God, thank you, God!"

It did not matter in that moment that the boy had done something he shouldn't have. They were just so relieved to have him home. They were overjoyed to have their little boy back.

That is how God loves us. His love for us is unconditional. No matter how much we may have messed up, He always welcomes us back.

I know I forget this often, and that is why I always come back to stillness. In stillness and quiet, I can remember who I truly am. I am not my fear or insecurities. I am not Monica, the angel. I am not Roma, the celebrity. I am Roma, God's beloved. No matter how far I have strayed or how much I may have forgotten, that identity never changes. Sometimes I feel far from God. Sometimes I feel close to God. But God is not the variable in that equation. I am. The illusion of separation is just that, an illusion. God is always there. I've just turned away and cannot see Him.

If we are all God's children, it means that we are all one family. If you have lived your life wondering where you belong, searching for home, it is here. We are all the family of God. We forget. We get caught up in separation. But we are all one family. We all belong to each other, like Mother Teresa taught. Like Maya Angelou showed us.

Remembering this will change everything.

So while we go out in the world, searching and searching and searching for home, it is within that we will find it. Our home is knowing that we are God's beloved children; and no matter how dark life can feel, He is always there to guide us, comfort us, and shelter us.

He is our home.

Thank you, God.

Ultimately the only way that I can be myself is to become identified with Him in Whom is hidden the reason and fulfillment of my existence.

THOMAS MERTON

It has always seemed to me, ever since early
childhood, that, amid all the commonplaces
of life, I was very near to a kingdom of ideal
beauty. Between it and me hung only a thin
veil. I could never draw it quite aside, but
sometimes a wind fluttered it and I caught
a glimpse of the enchanting realm beyond—
only a glimpse—but those glimpses have
always made life worthwhile.

Lucy Maud Montgomery

We are above all things loved—that is the good news of the gospel—and loved not just the way we turn up on Sundays in our best clothes and on our best behavior and with our best feet forward, but loved as we alone know ourselves to be, the weakest and shabbiest of what we are along with the strongest and gladdest. To come together as people who believe that just maybe this gospel is actually true should be to come together like people who have just won the Irish Sweepstakes. It should have us throwing our arms around each other like people who have just discovered that every single man and woman in those pews is not just another familiar or unfamiliar face but is our long-lost brother and our long-lost sister, because despite the fact that we have all walked in different gardens and knelt at different graves, we have all, humanly speaking, come from the same place and are heading out into the same blessed mystery that awaits us all.

Frederick Buechner

I'm sorry, God, for
forgetting the truth.
That you are my Father,
and I am your child.
That we all belong
to one family.
and that is where
we will find home.
Help us remember,
daily,
moment by moment,
our true identity
as yours.
always yours.
Forever yours.
That you are preparing
a place for us.
a place where all that
we've lost is now found.
a place where all is fulfilled,
nothing is lacking.
and we have you.
You.
always,
You.

Everything Is
Waiting for You

Your great mistake is to act the drama
as if you were alone. As if life
were a progressive and cunning crime
with no witness to the tiny hidden
transgressions. To feel abandoned is to deny
the intimacy of your surroundings. Surely,
even you, at times, have felt the grand array;
the swelling presence, and the chorus, crowding
out your solo voice. You must note
the way the soap dish enables you,
or the window latch grants you freedom.
Alertness is the hidden discipline of familiarity.
The stairs are your mentor of things

to come, the doors have always been there
to frighten you and invite you,
and the tiny speaker in the phone
is your dream-ladder to divinity.

Put down the weight of your aloneness and ease into
the conversation. The kettle is singing
even as it pours you a drink, the cooking pots
have left their arrogant aloofness and
seen the good in you at last. All the birds
and creatures of the world are unutterably
themselves. Everything is waiting for you.

David Whyte

YOU NEVER WALK ALONE

At the beginning of every episode of *Touched by an Angel*, they played our theme song. The lovely Della Reese sang it, and the themes it touched on were those that appeared on every show. It was called "Walk with You," and it told the story that no matter what, there was someone by your side. You were never alone. It could be an angel or God. But no matter what, there was someone there.

At the time, I don't think I even recognized how similar the themes in this song were to those in the song my mother sang to me, "You'll Never Walk Alone," and how similar they were to the theme of the poem "Footprints," which my father shared with me shortly after my mother's death. Over and over, the theme of my life story has been that we are never alone. Though I was an orphan in my early twenties, an age when most still want the guidance of their parents, I was never alone.

Here I am, so many years later, and that is still what I want to share.

Look for the butterflies. Look for the helpers. Look for the angels.

They are everywhere.

Our lives probably look very different—yours and mine. None of us traverses the same path. But I know that we all share one thing in common, and that is that our Father in heaven loves each of us equally and fiercely. He is forging a beautiful butterfly out of whatever cocoon you may be enduring.

Take heart. Have faith. And when the light comes, as it always does, enjoy the flight to the rest of your life.

I know that, one day, we will meet. It may be on this earth, but probably not. But I know we will meet in heaven.

I'll see you there.

Death is not extinguishing
the light; it is only
putting out the lamp
because the dawn has come.

RABINDRANATH TAGORE

So do not fear, for I am with you;
do not be dismayed, for I am your God.
I will strengthen you and help you;
I will uphold you with my righteous right hand.

ISAIAH 41:10 (NIV)

Walk with You

When you walk down the road
Heavy burden, heavy load

I will rise and I will walk with you
When you walk through the night
And you feel like you wanna just give up,
give up, give up on the fight
I will come and I will walk with you
Walk with you
Until the sun don't even shine
Walk with you
I'll be there all the time

I tell you I'll walk with you
See you through
When you walk from this place
And you gotta go to meet Him face to face
Take my hand and I will walk with you

Oh, oh walk with you
Till the clouds fade away
I tell you I'll walk with you
Each and every day

Oh yes I'll walk with you

Lyrics by Marc Lichtman,
additional lyrics by Martha Williamson
Theme song from *Touched by an Angel*

May

the road rise to meet you,
May the wind be always
at your back,
May the sun shine warm
upon your face,
The rains fall soft upon
your fields and,
Until we meet again,
May God hold you
in the palm of His hand.

IRISH BLESSING

Acknowledgments

My Angels along the Way

There have been countless people who have come into my life at times when I greatly needed them. I know these were angels sent by God to encourage and strengthen me. I am so fortunate to have been blessed by incredible friends, family, colleagues, and partners in my life, and this book wouldn't exist without them.

Gone but not forgotten, of course, are my precious mom and dad and my beloved Auntie Ruby.

Across the ocean in Derry, I thank my family for their constant love and support over the years: my brother Lawrence and his wife, Fiona; my half sisters Ann and Jacinta, and their husbands, John and Michael; my half brother Pat and his wife, Ann; my half brother Fr. John; our dear family friend Fr. Paddy O'Kane; and all my many nieces and nephews.

A thank-you to my lovely mother-in-law, Jean; I'm so grateful that she and her late husband, Archie, came into my life when I married Mark.

I thank friends and mentors and wise hearts along the way for enriching my life and helping me discover my gifts and giving me the courage to dream: my sincere thanks to Roy Grant, Sandra Freeman, and Faith O'Reilly for believing in me. To directors Jack Going, who gave me my first big theater break, and Larry Peerce, who gave me my first big television break. Who knows where I'd be without you!

Thank you to my beloved *Touched by an Angel* family. I am so grateful for the love we shared after so many wonderful years spent together: to

Martha Williamson and the cast and crew, in particular the late John Dye and my own beloved momma, Della Reese.

Thank you to all my *Bible* and *A.D.* family, the entire cast and crew who brought so much light to my life, and in particular Richard Bedser.

Thank you to Gary Barber and my MGM family and all of my Light-Workers family, who stay as committed as I am to telling positive and encouraging stories and trying to change the world through kindness, and especially to John Kilcullen and Katherine Warnock for their input on this book.

Thank you to all the folks at Operation Smile who volunteer to give of their time and talent, changing the world one smile at a time.

Thank you to everyone who helped with *Box of Butterflies*, breathing life into its pages with love and support and creativity. To Jan Miller and Shannon Marven for helping me find the right publisher for this project and your unwavering support throughout. To Pam Reynolds, Brian Edwards, and Christina Tajalli, for their legal expertise. To Judith Curr, Carolyn Reidy, Philis Boultinghouse, Stephen Fallert, Jonathan Merkh, and the entire team at Simon & Schuster and Howard Books. To Torrey Sharp and Min Choi for their beautiful design; Jetty Stutzman, Linda Medvene, and Austin Hargraves for their incredible work on the cover; and Lina Plath and Clareanne Darragh from Frank PR, my tireless PR team. To Cindy DiTiberio, who came alongside at just the right time to help me envision what this book could be, who helped me get the stories out of my heart and onto the page, and whose tireless dedication to the process has helped this book emerge into the beautiful treasure it is.

A special thanks to all the writers and contributors who granted me rights to use their material, which so greatly enhanced this book. They have been butterflies for me along the way, and I'm so grateful that I can share them with you. A special thanks to Mary Oliver, Martha Williamson and Marc Lichtman, Anne Neilson, Karen Kingsbury, Phil Coulter, David Whyte, and the dear Dr. Maya Angelou.

A thank-you to Ashley Chase, my invaluable assistant, who handles so many details and keeps me focused, on time, and on schedule.

I'm so grateful for the special friends who have graced my path. There are way too many to mention here, but in particular, I thank my girlfriends close to home and overseas, friends whom I can count on no matter what, my true angels along the way, including Joanna, Moira, Cynthia, Elizabeth, Carol and Kay, Irena, Brooke, Lisa, Marilyn, and Valerie.

I've been humbled and overwhelmed by the generosity of so many people and their kind words on behalf of *Box of Butterflies*. There has been so much support from friends, colleagues—people I so deeply admire and respect—and I am incredibly grateful. Given the immense response, I regret we were not able to print all of the gracious words offered. I thank each and every person listed below from the bottom of my heart and have created a special place where you can read everything that people have been saying about *Box of Butterflies* at www.boxofbutterflies.com.

My deepest thanks go to:

Megan Alexander, Moll Anderson, Raymond Arroyo, Pastors Caroline and Matthew Barnett, Pastor Luke Barnett, Bishop Robert Barron, Pastor Mark Batterson, Bob Beltz, Lisa Bevere, Rev. Msgr. J. Brian Bransfield, Bishop Dale C. Bronner, Brooke Burke-Charvet, Rev. William Byrne, Phil Cooke, LL COOL J, Jeremy and Jessica Courtney, Pastors David and Nicole Crank, Cindy Crawford, Laurie Crouch, Jim Daly, Juan Pablo Di Pace, Shannen Doherty, Fran Drescher, Joshua DuBois, Rev. Jonathan Falwell, Dr. Ronnie Floyd, Pastor Ken Foreman, Bob Goff, Kathie Lee Gifford, Archbishop José H. Gomez, Jon Gordon, Pastors Craig and Amy Groeschel, Pastor Bobby Gruenewald, Pastor John C. Hagee, Billy Hallowell, Michelle McKinney Hammond, Patricia Heaton, Pastors Bobbie and Brian Houston, Arianna Huffington, Dr. Joel C. Hunter, Jackelyn and Donald Iloff, Jerry Johnson, Jason Kennedy, Lauren Scruggs- Kennedy, Karen Kingsbury, Ali Landry, Pastor Max Lucado, Gabe and Rebekah Lyons, Dr. Bill and Kathy Magee, Pastor Erwin Raphael McManus, Santiago "Jimmy" Mellado, Dr. Carl A. Moeller, Johnnie Moore, Pastor Phil Munsey, Anne Neilson, Nancy O'Dell, Cardinal Seán O'Malley, Pastor Victoria Osteen, Dr. Mehmet Oz, Sister Rose Pacatte, Kevin Palau, Tony Robbins, Willie and Korie Robertson, Rev. Samuel Rodriguez, SQuire Rushnell, Rodrigo Santoro, Joel and Luke Smallbone, Pastor Judah Smith, Michael W. Smith, Pastors Andy and Sandra Stanley, Pastor Dave Stone, Cal Thomas, Pastor Brian Tome, Nick Vujicic, Pastor Holly Wagner, Pastor Rick and Kay Warren, and Cardinal Donald Wuerl.

Last but not least, I must thank my closest family. My own little Brady Bunch! I am so grateful to my beloved husband, Mark, my best friend, partner, soul mate, and the absolute love of my life. He is the true leading man in my life. Loving him and being loved by him is more than I could have ever dreamed of. I am grateful for the two amazing sons he brought into my life. I have cherished helping to raise James and Cameron, and I love them dearly and am so proud of the young men they have become.

And to Reilly, my beloved daughter: your birth blessed me more than you could ever know. You are a part of my heart, and loving you brings me so much joy. Thanks for being the best daughter a mother could have.

Credits

Every effort has been made to obtain permissions required for quoted material of a certain length in this work. If any required acknowledgments have been omitted, or any rights overlooked, it is unintentional. Please notify the publishers of any omissions, and they will be rectified in future editions.

Page x: "I Have Decided," from *A Thousand Mornings* by Mary Oliver, published by The Penguin Press New York. Copyright © 2012 by Mary Oliver. Reprinted by permission of the Charlotte Sheedy Literary Agency Inc.

Page 20: "You'll Never Walk Alone." Copyright © 1945 by Richard Rodgers and Oscar Hammerstein II. Copyright renewed. Williamson Music (ASCAP), an Imagem Company, owner of publication and allied rights throughout the world. International Copyright Secured. All Rights Reserved. Used by Permission.

Page 28: "He Will Cover You," by artist Ruth Chou Simons, GraceLaced.com

Pages 48–49: Excerpt(s), "Blessing: For Courage," from *To Bless the Space between Us*: *A Book of Blessings*, by John O'Donohue. Copyright © 2008 by John O'Donohue. Used by permission of Doubleday, an imprint of the Knopf Doubleday Publishing Group, a division of Penguin Random House LLC. All rights reserved. Any third-party use of this material, outside of this publication, is prohibited. Interested parties must apply directly to Penguin Random House LLC for permission. For the United Kingdom: Excerpts from *Benedictus* by John O'Donohue. Published by Bantam Press. Reprinted by per-

Benedictus by John O'Donohue. Published by Bantam Press. Reprinted by permission of The Random House Group Limited. © John O'Donohue 2007. Audio Rights: excerpted from *To Bless the Space Between Us*. Copyright © 2008 with permission of Sounds True Inc.

Page 110: Photo: Kevin Lynch, art direction by 30sixty Advertising, History®.

Pages 118–19: "My Little Angel."

Words and Music by Phil Coulter.

Copyright © 1999 Spirit Catalog Holdings, S.a.r.l.

All rights controlled and administered by Spirit Two Music, Inc.

International Copyright Secured. All Rights Reserved.

Reprinted by Permission of Hal Leonard LLC.

Pages 124–25: "Blessing: For a Mother-to-Be," from *To Bless the Space between Us: A Book of Blessings*, by John O'Donohue. Copyright © 2008 by John O'Donohue. Used by permission of Doubleday, an imprint of the Knopf Doubleday Publishing Group, a division of Penguin Random House LLC. All rights reserved. Any third-party use of this material, outside of this publication, is prohibited. Interested parties must apply directly to Penguin Random House LLC for permission. For the United Kingdom: Excerpts from *Benedictus* by John O'Donohue. Published by Bantam Press. Reprinted by permission of The Random House Group Limited. © John O'Donohue 2007. Audio Rights: excerpted from *To Bless the Space Between Us*. Copyright © 2008 with permission of Sounds True Inc.

Page 139: "Angels," original artwork by Anne Neilson, used by permission.

Pages 144–45: "Mary, Did You Know?" Mark Lowry/Buddy Greene. © 1991 Word Music (ASCAP), LLC, Rufus Music (ASCAP) (adm. at CapitolCMGPublishing.com). All Rights on behalf of Word Music, LLC, administered by WB Music Corp. International Copyright Secured. All Rights Reserved. Used by Permission.

Pages 150: "Touched by an Angel" aka "Love's Exquisite Freedom" by Maya Angelou. Copyright © 1975 by Maya Angelou. Reprinted by permission of Caged Bird Legacy, LLC.

Pages 164: "Praying," from the volume *Thirst*, by Mary Oliver, published by Beacon Press, Boston. Copyright © 2006 by Mary

Praise for *Box of Butterflies*

"Regardless of the season of life you are in, Roma Downey's hope-filled book powerfully reveals the love, grace, and kindness waiting for you in Christ. Roma warmly guides you through a reading experience that will build your faith, renew your mind, and encourage your heart. Open this book and prepare to be blessed as you experience God's grace in a new, fresh, and intimate way."

—Craig and Amy Groeschel, pastors, Life.Church, and authors, *From This Day Forward*

"We all need inspiration in our everyday lives to give us strength as we face obstacles, challenges, and setbacks. I am grateful that Roma offers such a beautiful compilation of so many wonderfully wise and thoughtful sentiments. Thank you, Roma. I am proud to call you a friend."

—Fran Drescher, author, actress, health advocate

"Equal parts deeply personal and profoundly inspirational, as you turn these pages you won't just find a story about Roma; this is a book about how God paints on the canvas of our lives with many beautiful colors. We have all experienced pain and loss, joy and celebration. You'll find words in this book that will lift you up."

—Bob Goff, author, *New York Times* bestseller *Love Does*

"In the time that we have known Roma, we have found her to be like a breath of sweet air from above. We are confident this book will enlarge your perception and revelation of a God who fails not. The imprint of His kindness and goodness is all around us, and Roma is certainly one capable and gifted in helping others to see it. *Box of Butterflies* is a testament of gratitude, offering comfort and assurance for the hungry soul."

—Bobbie and Brian Houston, global senior pastors, Hillsong Church

"Roma's beautiful soul shines through in *Box of Butterflies*, reminding us that despite the struggles and difficulties of life, God is always with us. Her personal stories, quotes, and words of encouragement will be the inspiration you need to remember God's presence and rediscover the beauty found in the life around you."

—Lisa Bevere, *New York Times* bestselling author and cofounder, Messenger International

"Every so often a person comes along who possesses that remarkable combination of passionate faith and natural authenticity, so much so that God can use them to change the world and transform hearts. Roma Downey is just that kind of person, and *Box of Butterflies* is a powerful reflection of her one-of-a-kind spirit."

—Rev. Samuel Rodriguez, president, National Hispanic Christian Leadership Conference

"Roma Downey releases a new kind of light. As she shares with us beautiful moments of her life story in these pages, it quickly becomes clear that Roma is giving us, with surpassing gentleness, the internal tools to navigate our own life stories. What *Touched by an Angel* was to television, *Box of Butterflies* is to books. You won't be able to read it just once."

—Rev. Msgr. J. Brian Bransfield, general secretary, United States Conference of Catholic Bishops

"In this moving book, Roma shares the source of the light she has been beaming to the world since she entered our lives in *Touched by an Angel*. Not one to deny the difficulty and darkness of the world, she recounts stories of her own losses and how she found courage and faith in difficult times. Thanks, Roma!"

—Andy and Sandra Stanley, authors, communicators, and founders, North Point Ministries, Alpharetta, Georgia

"*Box of Butterflies* celebrates the victory over life's struggles, providing us the encouragement to live life without limit! I encourage you to get several copies of this stunning book that provides a window into the serene majesty of God's creation."

—Pastor John C. Hagee, founder and senior pastor, Cornerstone Church, San Antonio, Texas

"There is a lot of pain in this world, and my friend Roma has not been a stranger to that. But she also knows that in the midst of life's trials there is hope—hope in a God who loves us and cares about every detail of our lives. This book will encourage you and bolster your faith."

—Jim Daly, president, Focus on the Family

"Thank you, Roma, for sharing your *Box of Butterflies* with us. I'm fortunate to count Roma as a friend—the kind of friend that inspires you to be your best self. Roma reminds us that life is a bumpy, wonderful and sometimes tragic journey, but our power comes from how we choose to face that journey. Roma lives a life full of faith and spirit, and you just can't help but be drawn in!"

—Cindy Crawford, model/businesswoman